Samuel Sharpe, Apostle Barnabas

Epistle of Barnabas

from the Sinaitic manuscript of the Bible

Samuel Sharpe, Apostle Barnabas

Epistle of Barnabas
from the Sinaitic manuscript of the Bible

ISBN/EAN: 9783337099992

Printed in Europe, USA, Canada, Australia, Japan

Cover: Foto ©Lupo / pixelio.de

More available books at **www.hansebooks.com**

ΒΑΡΝΑΒΑ ΕΠΙΣΤΟΛΗ.

THE EPISTLE OF BARNABAS

FROM THE

SINAITIC MANUSCRIPT OF THE BIBLE,

WITH A TRANSLATION,

BY

SAMUEL SHARPE.

WILLIAMS AND NORGATE:
14 HENRIETTA STREET, COVENT GARDEN, LONDON;
AND 20 SOUTH FREDERICK STREET, EDINBURGH.

1880.

PRINTED BY TAYLOR AND FRANCIS,
RED LION COURT, FLEET STREET.

PREFACE

The Epistle of Barnabas seems to claim notice in any Life of the Apostle Paul: first, because the two apostles had at one time lived in close friendship, and it in part explains why at a later time Paul's feelings towards Barnabas were changed; and secondly, because it offers the earliest example of the Gnosticism which was creeping into the Christian Churches, very much to the trouble of Paul. But when I wished to mention this Epistle in my work on "The Journeys and Epistles of the Apostle Paul," I was met with the difficulty of not knowing of any English translation that I thought satisfactory. Hence this publication.

S. S.

32 Highbury Place,
11th September, 1880.

INTRODUCTION.

Joses, who by the Apostles was surnamed Barnabas, was an Israelite of the island of Cyprus, and of the tribe of Levi. He is first mentioned in Acts iv. 36, as selling his land in Cyprus and laying the money at the Apostles' feet as a contribution to the young Church. We next hear of him as bringing Saul, who had lately been persecuting the Church, to the Apostles who distrusted him, and assuring them that Saul's conversion was real (Acts ix. 27). He next goes down from Jerusalem to Antioch to preach to the Church in that Greek city (Acts xi. 22). He then goes to Tarsus in search of Saul, and brings him to Antioch to join in preaching there (Acts xi. 25). When the Church of Antioch sends money to the relief of the poor of Jerusalem, they send it by the hands of Barnabas and Saul (Acts xi. 30). He then accompanies Saul on his first missionary journey (Acts xiii. 3). Up to this time, of the two friends Barnabas had been the chief; he had been the longest time a Christian, and he was probably the older man. From this only can we form an opinion of his age.

If we suppose that Saul, now called Paul, was about 22 years old when he is called a young man, at the time of Stephen's martyrdom, in A.D. 40, he may have been born in A.D. 18; and we may by conjecture suppose that Barnabas was born as early as A.D. 15 or earlier, and therefore was at least 55 years old when Jerusalem was destroyed and our Epistle probably written. When Paul and Barnabas travel together they are both called Apostles in Acts xiv. 14.

The last we know of Barnabas in the New Testament is in the Epistle to the Colossians, when Paul, having occasion to mention Mark, describes him as the cousin or nephew of Barnabas, adding " about whom ye have received commands; if he come to you, receive him." Thus Paul had sent to the Colossians some private warning against Barnabas's teaching, which he had latterly found reasons for disliking. From his Greek education in Cyprus we might suppose that Barnabas had adopted something of the Alexandrian philosophy, which no doubt was the character of Apollos's teaching. He probably was a ready speaker, as we judge from his new name—Barnabas, or *Son of exhortation*. As a Levite he is likely to have had a full acquaintance with the Scriptures, but, from the place of his birth, perhaps in Greek rather than in Hebrew. This is nearly all that we can know of him before reading the Epistle which bears his name.

From the Epistle we shall learn that when Nero's persecution of the Christians broke out, in A.D. 64, Barnabas was able to save his life by withdrawing to some place of safety, which he does not think proper to name; and that from thence, in the beginning of Vespasian's reign, he was able to write to the flock among whom he had been ministering before the persecution.

This Epistle scholars have lately very much put aside as not being the work of Paul's companion, but, as I consider, without good reason. The evidence for and against cannot be better stated than in the words of Drs. Roberts and Donaldson in the preface to their translation:—

"External and internal evidence here come into direct collision. The ancient writers who refer to this Epistle unanimously attribute it to Barnabas the Levite of Cyprus, who held such an honourable place in the infant church. Clement of Alexandria does so again and again (Strom. ii. 6, ii. 7, etc.). Origen describes it as 'a catholic epistle' (Cont. Cels. i. 63), and seems to rank it among the Sacred Scriptures (Comm. in Rom. i. 24). Other statements have been quoted from the fathers, to show that they held this to be an authentic production of the apostolic Barnabas; and certainly no other name is ever hinted at in Christian antiquity as that of the writer. But notwithstanding this, the internal evidence is now generally regarded as conclusive against this opinion. On perusing the Epistle the reader will be in circumstances to judge of this matter for himself. He will be led to consider whether the spirit and tone of the writing, as so decidedly opposed to all respect for Judaism—the numerous inconsistencies which it contains with regard to Mosaic enactments and observances—the absurd and trifling interpretations of Scripture which it suggests—and the many silly vaunts of superior knowledge in which its writer indulges—can possibly comport with its ascription to the fellow-labourer of St. Paul."

Thus these translators find nothing in the Epistle which leads them to think it not genuine, except, 1st, its want of respect for Judaism, which, however, is not remarkable in the friend of Paul; 2nd, its inaccuracy as to the Mosaic law, which is certainly a proof of an imperfect education but no proof that it was not written by Barnabas; 3rd, its trifling interpretations of Scripture, in which it is by no means singular among the writings of the time, as in those of the learned Philo; and, 4th, its silly vaunts of superior knowledge, which is exactly the failing which we should expect to find in any Greek Jew who had fallen into the conceited Gnosticism of that age. Upon the whole there is nothing whatever to be said against the genuineness of this Epistle, except that it falls far short of the high excellence that we should wish to find in any writing which puts forth a claim from the name of its author to be admitted into the canon of the New Testament.

One reason given for doubting the authenticity of the Epistle is that in ch. v. he says that Jesus, when choosing his Apostles who were to preach the Good Tidings, chose "those who were $ανομωτεροι$, *impious* [or, rather, *neglectors of the Law*, in matters important], above all sin," in order to show that he came "to call not the righteous but sinners." This has been understood to mean that he calls the Apostles impious; and therefore that he could not have been Barnabas. If, however, this argument were good, the words would prove that the writer could not have been a Christian; and hence the argument is very clearly of no weight. Moreover the words do not necessarily bear that meaning; and the writer's aim throughout the Epistle is so obviously to show his cleverness in handling Scripture, that we need not so understand them.

When the Apostles at the Council (Acts xv.) consented to waive much of the Mosaic Law in favour of Gentile converts, they certainly were neglectors of the Law; and Barnabas's words do not necessarily mean more, although by the fancifully applying to the call of the twelve Apostles the text, "he came to call not the righteous but sinners," the words would be so understood in any less fanciful writer.

In considering the authorship of the Epistle we must have regard to Paul's words in Coloss. iv. 10. There he says very clearly that he had written a private letter, or had sent a message of commands, to the Colossians about Barnabas. This cannot have been otherwise than something that he would not mention in the public Epistle, some warning against listening to Barnabas's teaching. We thus have reasonable proof that Paul at that time did not like Barnabas's opinions; and as Cyprus, of which island Barnabas was a native, was much under the influence of Alexandria, we might guess, without the evidence of this Epistle, that it was Barnabas's leaning towards Gnosticism that displeased Paul.

The Epistle is important in the history of Paul. It shows

what Barnabas was; it explains how it was that when starting in missionary work as Paul's superior he soon fell into the second place; and it justifies Paul for warning the Colossians against him. Moreover it does much to explain the difficulties which met Paul on the side of the Græcizing Jews, while on the other side he was struggling against the ceremonialism of the Jewish disciples who shunned the Greeks.

We can only approve of the judgment of the early Christians, who while acknowledging this Epistle as the work of Barnabas, thought it not worthy of a place in the New Testament. Had it been limited to the last four chapters, we should gladly have seen it standing beside the other Apostolic Epistles. Those latter chapters can alone be profitably read for religious instruction.

But notwithstanding the want of judgment and the conceit shown by Barnabas in his explanation of the Scriptures, this Epistle is a valuable addition to the scanty literature of the Apostolic times. It seems to have been written after the Epistles of Paul and James, after the Book of Revelation, but before any of the other Epistles. It is probably the only Christian work remaining outside of the New Testament which was written while the books of the New Testament were being written, except the Wisdom of Solomon in the Apocrypha. That was written before Barnabas's Epistle, and may indeed be the earliest Christian writing remaining to us; but its value is lessened by our not knowing the name and circumstances of the writer. There are many things in the New Testament which we should understand better if we had more contemporary Christian writings. Even if they were of little value of themselves for religious instruction, yet they would be of the greatest value as offering us examples of style, of the use of words, and of modes of thought, for comparison with the New Testament. The Epistle of Clement, bishop of Rome, addressed to the Corinthian Church, belongs to a later generation. It was written probably about A.D. 95; and the writer must not be taken for the Clement mentioned in Philipp. iv. 3, who was a fellow worker with Paul at Philippi nearly forty years before, in A.D. 57 or earlier.

The chief peculiarities in the Epistle of Barnabas are:—

1st. The writer's fondness for a strained interpretation of Scripture; as in finding that the world would come to an end in six thousand years from the creation, because it was made in six days. Yet more fanciful is the finding the Greek name of Jesus and his cross in Abraham's 318 servants, taking the first two letters in his name, III, as the Greek numerals for 18, and for the cross using the letter T, the Greek numeral for 300. We notice the same peculiarity in a less degree in the Epistle to the Hebrews, where in vii. 6 Levi is said to have paid tithes through Abraham. Paul also is not wholly free from this, as when in Gal. iv. he compares the Jews to Abraham's children through the bondwoman, and the Christians to his children through his wife Sarah.

In this matter Philo seems to have been the great misleader of his generation, by the forced allegories with which he ventures to explain the Bible. Barnabas had no doubt read his writings; and he so far copies him as often to introduce his fanciful explanation of a text by a question, such "What is the meaning of these words?"

2nd. A conceited claim to superior knowledge, and to the possession of "the Knowledge," or Gnosticism. It was against this conceit that Paul warns the Corinthians in 1 Cor. viii. and warns Timothy in 1 Tim. vi. 20. But Barnabas's Gnosticism does not partake of the mischievous opinions which troubled Paul in the Corinthian church, and at a later time in the Asiatic churches.

3rd. A strong dislike for Judaism and the Jews, while every part of the Epistle shows that he was himself of Hebrew birth and of Jewish or rather Græco-Jewish education. But we must remember that this dislike was as much political as religious. A Levite of Cyprus, when he came up to Jerusalem, was probably treated as an inferior by the proud priests of Jerusalem; and like the Israelites of Galilee, and the common people of Judea, he may naturally have felt some jealousy against that upper portion of the nation who claimed to be the only true Jews. This was shown in the fate of Jesus, whom the common people, his admirers, followed in crowds, while the Jews said "Crucify him." It had been equally shown four centuries earlier, when the people of Jerusalem came up complaining to Nehemiah the Pacha, with "a great cry against their brethren the Jews" (Nehem. v. 1). But in his dislike of

Judaism Barnabas goes beyond the Apostle Paul. Paul advised the Gentiles not to come under circumcision (Gal. v. 2); but Barnabas wishes the practice to be abolished altogether. In a time of revolution, whether political or religious, opinions change very fast; and Barnabas was writing this seven years after the latest of Paul's Epistles, and fifteen years since Paul had written about Judaism.

4th. There are many peculiar thoughts and words the same as in the New Testament. Of the words, we have in ch. xiii. του μεταξυ *the future*, as in Acts xiii. 42, το μεταξυ *the next*. There are also some few words which are not there found. Such are

ὁ Μακροθυμος, *the Forbearing one*, a name for God, ch. iii.

ὁ Μελας, *the Black one*, the Devil, ch. iv. and xx.

επιλυτος, perhaps for επηλυτος, *a proselyte*, in a bad sense, one who had fallen away from Christianity, ch. iii. A pervert rather than a convert.

μοναζω, *to live alone*, as a monk, ch. iv.

The Eighth Day, meaning the first day of the week, ch. xv.

The Holy Age, meaning the life after death, ch. x.

The Vessel of the Spirit, a name for Christ when in the flesh, ch. vii. and xi.

The Excellent or Noble Vessel, the same, ch. xxi.

5th. The Greek is very faulty. The indicative mood is often used for the subjunctive, and the present tense for the future. These are Hebraisms, and they sometimes lead to obscurity, as in ἑως εστι, which I venture to render *until it shall be*, thus, " until the excellent Vessel [the body of Christ] shall be with you," ch. xxi. *This* I understand to mean "Until the second coming of Christ."

Drs. Roberts and Donaldson render it "While you are in this fair vessel."

Other Hebraisms are:—

ακοη ακουσατω, *let him carefully* hear, ch. ix.

μνεια μνημονευετε, *remember carefully*, ch. xxi.

ει . . . ει, *whether* . . . *or*, ch. xiii., like אם . . . אם.

αφ' ών, *from where*, ch. iv. and xxi., like מ אשר.

For the numeral Seven he writes in ch. xv. εζ, or in the MS. EZ, not the simple letter Z. Hence we may suppose that Ez, not Zeta, was his name for the latter; as we form names for F, L, M, N, R, S, and X, by the help of a foregoing vowel.

Before the discovery of the Sinaitic manuscript of the Bible by Tischendorf we possessed no perfect copy of this Epistle in the original Greek. The first four chapters and a half were known only in an ancient Latin version. Since Tischendorf published his facsimile of the MS. several editions of this Epistle have appeared, such as one by Dressel in 1863, and one by Hilgenfeld in 1866. These editors in forming their texts have made use of other MSS. also, and of the Latin version; but in the following pages the text is strictly given as it appears in the Sinaitic MS.

This MS. was corrected throughout by a second hand, probably as soon as it was written. These corrections Tischendorf has carefully noted; and I have adopted them as being the text. The words are often badly spelt, which in the case of the diphthongs, and in them alone, I have ventured to correct; as the scribe has often written ι for ει, and ε for αι, and the reverse. These departures from the MS. I have noted in the margin, while all other seeming faults are left uncorrected. I have never ventured on any conjectures in order to make the quotations better agree with the Septuagint, or to make the words more probable. Thus I leave in ch. v. that on Jesus preaching to Israel "they greatly loved him," not, as some have read, "he loved them." Barnabas may have been thinking of the common people who heard him gladly, not of the Jews who put him to death. I have made no note of where contractions are used in the MS. except in one case, in ch. vii., where we have το θυσιαν. This, I consider, not a mistake, but a contraction for το θυσιαστηριον, and I have mentioned it in the margin, together with one or two conjectural emendations, to which I am driven by the needs of the translation, but which I have not introduced into the text.

While adding capital letters, stops, and the customary division of the Epistle into chapters, I have also added the aspirate and the *Iota subscriptum* to those vowels which usually receive them from the printer.

This MS. of our Epistle is important on two accounts: first, because the Epistle there stands as part of the Bible following immediately upon the Book of Revelation, and thereby receives a strong testimony to its genuineness; and secondly, because it gives us in ch. iv. a few words which help us towards a date of when the Epistle was written. These words had been omitted in the ancient Latin version, perhaps because the writer could give no meaning to them. Tischendorf also seems to have found a difficulty in them, as he puts a note upon them to say that they are uncorrected by the corrector of the MS. Dressel repeats Tischendorf's note, and in his Prolegomena further remarks that the Epistle makes no mention of persecutions, which is the very thought which I find in these words, and from which we may gain a date. Hilgenfeld also in his edition, and Drs. Roberts and Donaldson in their translation, consider the Greek here incorrect and unintelligible. There is a second passage near the end of the Epistle, which helps to explain the first; but in this also these scholars find a difficulty.

The first passage is in ch. iv. and is as follows (p. 10):— "And wishing to write many things to you, not as a teacher, but as one who loveth, I have hastened to write to you αφ' ὧν, *from* [*places*] *which* εχομεν, *we purpose* not to leave. Therefore προσεχομεν, *we notice* your defilement in the last days. For the whole time of your faith will profit you nothing, unless now in this wicked time, and in the coming difficulties, we oppose ourselves as becometh sons of God, so that the Black one should gain no sly entrance." Here we may take αφ' ὧν as a Hebraism, and compare it to מ אשר, *from where*; for the Hebrew pronoun has the force of *where*, as well as *who*; or we may compare it to Homer's ἐξ οὗ, *from* [*the time*] *when*, Il. i. 6. To εχομεν we may give a not unusual intransitive sense, as, *we have a mind, we hold ourselves*, or *we purpose*; and see in ch. vii. and xv. προσεχετε, *do ye notice*, followed as here by an accusative case.

The second passage is in ch. xxi. (p. 62), thus: "Therefore I have the rather hastened to write, in order to cheer you, ἀφ' ὧν, *from* [*places*] *where* I was able to be safe."

These passages are so far important that I add the translation proposed by Drs. Roberts and Donaldson, which they at the same time acknowledge is very unsatisfactory. They render the first of these passages as follows:—

"Now, being zealous to write many things to you, not as your teacher, but as becometh one who loves you, I have taken care not to fail to write to you from what I myself possess, with a view to your purification. We take earnest heed in these last days; for the whole [past] time &c." And to this they add the following Note. "The Greek is here incorrect and unintelligible; and as the Latin omits the clause, our translation is merely conjectural. Hilgenfeld's text, if we give somewhat a peculiar meaning to ἐλλιπεῖν, may be translated, 'but as it is becoming in one who loves you not to fail in giving you what we have, I, though the very offscouring of you, have been eager to write to you.'"

The second passage they render thus:—"Wherefore I have been the more earnest to write to you, as my ability served, that I might have to cheer you. Farewell, &c." They read σώζεσθαι, *to be safe*, as being meant for σώζεσθε, *fare ye well*.

These translators agree with Tischendorf, Dressel, and Hilgenfeld in thinking the Greek of the first passage incorrect and corrupt; whereas I venture to think that the difficulty arises wholly from Barnabas choosing to write guardedly and obscurely, because during the persecution it was not safe for him to write about himself otherwise. Paul wrote several Epistles from his prison in Rome; but he is careful to say nothing about the treatment that he received; nor does he in the later Epistles venture to describe his trial and his release. Such was the caution necessary in those "evil times." The First Epistle of Peter and the Epistle to the Hebrews are equally guarded in speaking of the persecution.

The falling-off of the flock to whom the Epistle to the Hebrews was written is very slightly but severely mentioned: "Though by this time ye ought to be teachers, ye have again need of one to teach you what are the first principles of the oracles of God; and ye are become such as have need of milk, and not of strong meat" (Heb. v. 12). Peter writing from Babylon to churches in Asia Minor did not know how those flocks had acted in the difficulty, and says, "Rejoice ye, having just now for a short time, if need be, been made to grieve in manifold temptations, so that your faith when tried, &c." (1 Peter, i. 6).

Though the persecution of the Christians by Nero was carried on in Rome with great cruelty, and many suffered a torturing death, yet in other parts of the empire humanity softened the severity. All men are not brave enough to be martyrs; all men are not clear enough in their opinions to feel it a duty to suffer for them; and when the easy alternative was offered of escaping death by painting some Pagan emblem "the mark of the Beast" on the forehead or right hand, as said in Rev. xiii. 16, we may be sure that the larger number availed themselves of it. But there were others yet more fortunate, whose Christianity was not known to those in power, and who thus escaped unquestioned. These, who so escaped the notice of the persecutors, were probably the humbler portion of the church; while those who were more wealthy, and more in sight, had to defile themselves if they would escape martyrdom; and in ch. xix. Barnabas, having an eye to this, says "Thou shall not accept persons when reproving any one for falling off."

From the above sentences, if our translation is right, we gain some new facts in ecclesiastical history. We learn that in a time of persecution, probably that by Nero, in which Paul was put to death, Barnabas had escaped to some place of safety, as Peter, Mark, and Silas had fled to Babylon (1 Peter v. 12). From his place of retreat Barnabas wrote this Epistle to his Christian flock at the first moment that he was able. Many of his flock, not having been able in the same way to retire from the persecution, had saved their lives by consenting to some outward act of idolatry. This sacrifice of principle Barnabas calls their "defilement." With the same figure of speech the Writer of Revelation says, in iii. 4, of those who had not fallen off from the faith, "Thou hast a few names in Sardis which have not defiled their garments."

From ch. xvi. of our Epistle we learn that the Temple of Jerusalem was in the hands of the Romans, if not already destroyed. The capture took place in the second year of Vespasian, A.D. 70. Therefore the Epistle was not written before that time.

Moreover Barnabas quotes from Isaiah xlix. 17 in the Septuagint, a prophecy written on the return of the Jews from the captivity in Babylon, "They who have destroyed the Temple shall themselves build it up;" and he adds his own prophecy, "because of their going to war it was destroyed by the enemies, and now they [the Jews], and the servants of the enemies, shall build it up again." This was a bold prophecy; but Barnabas had some grounds for it, in Titus's anxiety to save the Temple as an ornament to his conquest, and in his repeated orders given to his soldiers to that purpose, as recorded by Josephus. Probably the orders for the complete destruction of the Temple were not given immediately on its being taken. Titus may have waited to learn Vespasian's opinion on the matter; and thus Barnabas may have been left for some little time in the belief that the Romans would rebuild it.

The active persecution of the Christians had ceased on Nero's death in A.D. 68, and even a year earlier in those places where Vespasian his lieutenant was in power; for Vespasian seems to have given little countenance to persecution. When the war broke out in Judea, the Romans learnt the difference between Jews and Christians, and they fought only against those "who had not the seal of God on their foreheads" (Rev. ix. 4). As the Christians did not take up arms, they were let alone. But as Barnabas, even two years later, when Jerusalem had been taken by Vespasian's lieutenant Titus, had not thought it safe to leave his unknown place of retreat, we judge that the cruel law against the Christians was not an edict which was to die with the emperor, but was a law by the senate, which remained in force until it was repealed. Any zealous prefect or proconsul was at liberty to make use of this law; yet as Vespasian was emperor in A.D. 69, and did not countenance religious persecution, and Barnabas says that he hastened to write his Epistle as soon as he safely could, we need not place it later than A.D. 70.

Again, near the beginning of ch. iv. we have the prophecy in Daniel vii. 7, 8, made use of rather violently to tell us that in the reign of Vespasian the world was soon to come to an end. The fourth Beast, wicked and strong above all the Beasts of the earth, is here meant for the Roman monarchy, although in Daniel it was the Greek monarchy. Out of it came ten horns, one of which was a little horn, a side-sprout, which humbled three great horns. This is Vespasian, who followed Galba, Otho, and Vitellius. At no later time could a Roman emperor so properly be called a side-sprout as when the empire had been for a century governed by one family, and when a ruler of a new family had come to the throne.

Here Barnabas is in part following the Book of Revelation, where Vespasian and his son Titus are called the sixth and seventh kings, while Galba, Otho, and Vitellius are passed over (Rev. xvii. 10). Thus, if those three are to be counted, Vespasian is the ninth; and Barnabas does not say that Vespasian was the tenth, but one of the ten; both writers speak of Titus's succession as assured.

In the first chapter Barnabas says that he hastened to send his advice κατα μικρον, *little by little*, meaning perhaps to send several short Epistles. But he may not at once have had the means of sending; and the Epistle shows traces of having been several months in hand. Thus, in the early chapters he is satisfied with the spiritual condition of his flock, and the times are evil, he that worketh has got the power [Nero is emperor]; but in chapter iv. he has heard of his flock's defilement [by idolatry], and Vespasian is on the throne; and again in ch. xvi. the Temple of Jerusalem is in the hands of the Romans.

The date of the Epistle is important, as showing how early the open profession of Gnosticism, or the boast of superior *knowledge*, had appeared within the Church. It is a justification of Paul's warning Timothy (1 Tim. vi. 20), and the Colossians (Col. ii.) against the "enticing words," and that seductive form of thought, which was soon to break out into open heresy, and to lead to a separation (1 John ii. 19). Barnabas himself shows none of those mischievous opinions which usually accompanied his line of thought, and which had appeared within the church of Corinth (1 Cor. vii., viii.), and which go far towards undermining morality. But perhaps we see something of the Gnostic admiration of the pagan philosophy, and thence the wish to rest good conduct and our happiness on the understanding rather than on the love of God, when he says in ch. i., "Righteousness of judging is the beginning; and the end is Love, Cheerfulness, and the witness of Joyfulness of works done in righteousness." These words Drs. Roberts and Donaldson omit from their translation, and say in a note, "The Greek is here totally unintelligible; it seems impossible either to punctuate it or construe it." Perhaps while noting how the same words, "beginning and end," were used in the foregoing line, these translators did not try the effect of a semicolon after the word "beginning," and of introducing a verb into each half of the sentence. We here see the obscurity in which the early writers often left their works for want of punctuation. Well might the Ethiopian say to Philip, of a passage in Isaiah, "How can I understand unless some one guide me?" (Acts viii. 31).

Another interesting passage is in ch. xix. "Thou shalt pacify those that fight, bringing them together; [God] will recognize it in thy sins." These last words Drs. Roberts and Donaldson render "Thou shalt confess thy sins." They possibly are following a different text.

The Epistle marks a step in the exaltation of Jesus which had been taking place in the minds of his disciples ever since the Crucifixion. In the introduction to the Fourth Gospel we read that the Word was with God at the beginning, and was an instrument in the creation of all things; and then that the Word became flesh and dwelt in the body of Jesus. So Barnabas, in chs. vii. and xi. styles Jesus the Vessel which contained the Spirit; and in ch. v. he puts forth more clearly the doctrine of his pre-existence, saying, that the Lord who suffered for us was present at the creation, when God said to him, "Let us make man after our image."

In Matt. xxiv. 22, the disciples are promised that the days will be shortened so that the Son of Man may come the sooner; and Barnabas says in ch. iv. that the days have been shortened that the Lord might come the sooner to his inheritance; and in ch. xxi. that the Lord is at hand with his reward, and that the day is at hand when the Evil one will perish.

The Epistle also tells us in ch. iv. that the Christian Sabbath was already kept on the eighth day, the day on which Jesus rose from the dead. This confirms what we learn from 1 Cor. xvi. 2, Acts xx. 7, and Rev. i. 10, as to Sunday being fixed upon as the Christian Sabbath.

The quotations from the Old Testament are numerous, probably all from the Septuagint, not from the Hebrew. But they are made very carelessly, and applied very fancifully, as the writer was guided by a conceited belief in his own Knowledge, γνωσις, which he sometimes calls ἡ γνωσις, *Gnosticism*. He also quotes the Book of Enoch, and the Book of Wisdom, and once introduces a passage which we find in Matthew's Gospel, with the important words, " as it is written." But this, as also several other thoughts which we find in that Gospel, may have been taken from the Logia, or Sayings of Jesus, a work mentioned by Justin Martyr, and which was in circulation before any one of the

Gospels was written. We have also thoughts which might have been borrowed from Paul's Epistles, from James, from Hebrews, from the Book of Revelation, and from John's Gospel. All these are noted at the foot of our pages. Many may not have been quotations from any book; they may have been thoughts floating among the Disciples by tradition; but it seems probable that the writer had at least read the Sayings of Jesus and several of Paul's Epistles. Indeed every page of our Epistle reminds us of Paul's writings. This is not remarkable, as Barnabas and Paul had at one time lived in great intimacy; and the stronger and better educated mind of Paul naturally impressed itself on that of Barnabas.

In ch. xxi. Barnabas speaks of "the judgments of the Lord, such as have been written." This would seem to mean a collection of speeches, as the Logia, rather than one of the Gospels; but that Barnabas had read John's Gospel is also probable, though the reasons for so thinking do not amount to a proof. His Epistle shows few signs of original thought, except indeed in his foolish conceits and far-fetched interpretations of passages in the Hebrew Scriptures. When therefore we find thoughts in the Epistle the same as those in the Fourth Gospel, and for which we know of no other source, we are led to trace them to that Gospel as to the original.

In the Introduction to John's Gospel we have two beginnings spoken of. In verse 1 we read, " In the beginning [of this new dispensation] the Word was with God ;" and in verse 2, "The same was with God in the [first] beginning." So in ch. vi. Barnabas says God " has accomplished a second fashioning [or a new creation] in these last days. The Lord says, Behold I make the last like the first."

That John, in the above words, is referring to Gen. i. 3, where God *spake the word*, and said, "Let there be light," is evident from his comparing, in verse 4, the spiritual Life of this second creation to the visible Light of the first creation. But Barnabas does not receive these words of John as meaning that God *spake the word*; and in ch. v. he refers them to Gen. i. 26, and thus makes God *speak to the Word* when he says "Let us make man in our own image." That Barnabas thus departs somewhat from John's meaning is strictly in accord with the way in which he handles the texts of the Old Testament, namely, with an evident wish to find a new meaning which the words did not originally bear. But at the same time the words of Barnabas are useful as a commentary on those of John.

That John's Gospel was already written and that Barnabas had read it receives some support from the probability that it is also made use of in the Book of Revelation, which was written in A.D. 69, one or two years earlier than our Epistle. Thus in Rev. xix. 13, we read, "His name is called The Word of God," a name which Jesus received, so far as we know, from the Introduction to John's Gospel. Again, in Rev. v. 6, he is described as "a Lamb standing as though slain." This also may be borrowed from John i. 29, where the Baptist says of him,

"Behold the Lamb of God, who taketh away the sin of the world."

Though we cannot overlook the faults of this Epistle arising from the writer's conceit of his superior knowledge, we may dwell with pleasure on much good advice which it contains; such as, that we should receive the difficulties which come upon us as good, for nothing comes to pass without God; Night and day we should remember the day of judgment; and We should make search to learn what are the things that God requires of us.

32, Highbury Place.
July 21, 1880.

ΒΑΡΝΑΒΑ ΕΠΙΣΤΟΛΗ.

THE EPISTLE OF BARNABAS.

THE EPISTLE OF BARNABAS.

Hail in peace, ye sons and daughters, in the name of the Lord who loved us.

Since God's acts of justification upon you have been many and rich, I rejoice beyond any thing and overabundantly over your happy and glorious spirits, that from Him ye have received grace as the graft of the spiritual gift. / Therefore I also rejoice rather in myself, hoping to be saved, because I truly see in you a spirit poured upon you from the Lord who is rich in love; thus the longed-for sight of you has greatly struck me about you. / Being therefore persuaded of this also, and being convinced in myself, that having spoken many things among you I am assured that the Lord hath travelled with me in the way of righteousness; and I myself am altogether forced into this loving of you above my own soul, because a great faith and love dwells in you by a hope of the life [promised] by Him.

Therefore considering this, that if I should be careful about you to communicate some part of what I have received, there will be to me a payment for having been of service to such souls, I have hastened to send to you little by little, so that together with your faith ye should have your knowledge perfect.

ΒΑΡΝΑΒΑ ΕΠΙΣΤΟΛΗ.

ΧΑΙΡΕΤΕ υἱοι και θυγατερες εν ονοματι Κυριου του αγαπησαντος ἡμας εν ειρηνῃ¹.

Μεγαλων μεν οντων και πλουσιων των του Θεου δικαιωματων εις ὑμας, ὑπερ τι και καθ᾽ ὑπερβολην ὑπερευφραινομαι² επι τοις μακαριοις και ενδοξοις ὑμων πνευμασιν, οὑ το εμφυτον της δωρεας πνευματικης χαριν ειληφατε³. Διο και μαλλον συνχαιρω εμαυτῳ, ελπιζων σωθηναι, ὁτι αληθως βλεπω εν ὑμιν εκκεχυμενον απο του πλουσιου της αγαπης Κυριου πνευμα εφ᾽ ὑμας· οὑτω με εξεπληξεν επι ὑμων ἡ επιποθητη οψις ὑμων. Πεπεισμενος⁴ ουν τουτο, και συνειδως⁵ εμαυτῳ ὁτι εν ὑμιν λαλησας πολλα επισταμαι ὁτι εμοι συνωδευσεν εν ὁδῳ δικαιοσυνης Κυριος, και παντως αναγκαζομαι⁶ κἀγω εις τουτο αγαπαν ὑμας ὑπερ την ψυχην μου, ὁτι μεγαλη πιστις και αγαπη εγκατοικει εν ὑμιν ελπιδι⁷ ζωης αυτου.

Λογισαμενος ουν τουτο ὁτι εαν μεληση μοι περι ὑμων του μερος τι μεταδουναι αφ᾽ οὑ ελαβον, ὁτι εσται μοι τοιουτοις πνευμασιν ὑπηρετησαντι εις μισθον, εσπουδασα κατα μικρον ὑμιν πεμπειν, ἱνα μετα της πιστεως ὑμων τελειαν⁸ εχητε⁹ την γνωσιν.

In MS.:—¹ ιρηνη. ² υπερευφρενομε. ³ ειληφαται. ⁴ πεπισμενος. ⁵ συνιὡς. ⁶ αναγκαζομε. ⁷ ελπιδει. ⁸ τελιαν. ⁹ εχηται.

There are therefore three things taught by the Lord, Life [hereafter], Faith, Hope; they are our beginning and end. And also Righteousness of judging is the beginning; and the end is Love, Cheerfulness, and the witness of Joyfulness of works done in righteousness. For the Almighty made known to us through the prophets the things which are past, and those which are beginning; and of those which are to come he has given to us the first fruits of the taste, of which things we, looking at them one by one as they are effected, ought, as he said, to press forward more richly and more loftily unto the fear of him. And I, not as a teacher, but as one of yourselves, will set forth a few things by which in the present state of affairs ye may be gladdened.

ii.] Therefore, since the days are evil, and he that worketh has got the power, we ought to give heed to ourselves, and to seek for the acts of justification by the Lord. The helps therefore of our faith are Fear, Patience, and moreover Long-suffering and Self-restraint, which fight for us. While these things remain, those things which are pure in relation to the Lord, and rejoice together with them, are Wisdom, Understanding, Science, Knowledge.

For He has made manifest to us through all the prophets that He has no need of sacrifices or burnt offerings or oblations, saying at one time indeed, "What is the multitude of your sacrifices to me? saith the Lord; I am full of burnt offerings; and I do not wish for the fat of rams, and the blood of bullocks and goats, not even when ye come to appear before me; for who hath required these of your hands? Nor shall ye continue to walk my court, not even if ye should bring a vain offering of fine flour. Incense is an abomination to me; your new-moon days and sabbaths I cannot bear."

Τρια ουν δογματα εστιν Κυριου, Ζωη, Πιστις, Ελπις, αρχη και τελος ημων. Και Δικαιοσυνη¹ κρισεως αρχη και τελος, Αγαπη, Ευφροσυνη, και Αγαλλιασεως εργων εν δικαιοσυναις μαρτυρια. Εγνωρισεν γαρ ημιν ο Δεσποτης δια των προφητων τα παρεληλυθοτα και τα ενεστωτα, και των μελλοντων δους απαρχας ημιν γευσεως, ων τα καθ' εκαστα βλεποντες ενεργουμενα, καθως ελαλησεν, οφειλομεν ² πλουσιωτερον και υψηλοτερον προσαγειν τω φοβω αυτου. Εγω δε ουκ ως διδασκαλος, αλλ' ως εις εξ υμων υποδειξω³ ολιγα δι' ων εν τοις παρουσιν ευφρανθησεσθε.

ii.] Ἡμερων ουν ουσων πονηρων, και αυτου του ενεργουντος εχοντος την εξουσιαν, οφειλομεν⁴ εαυτοις προσεχειν και εκζητειν τα δικαιωματα Κυριου. Της ουν πιστεως ημων εισιν βοηθοι, Φοβος, Ὑπομονη, ταδε συν μαχουντα ημιν Μακροθυμια και Εγκρατεια⁵. Τουτων μενοντων, τα προς Κυριον αγνως συνευφραινονται⁶ αυτοις Σοφια, Συνεσις, Επιστημη, Γνωσις.

Πεφανερωκεν γαρ ημιν δια παντων των προφητων οτι ουτε θυσιων, ουτε ολοκαυτωματων, ουτε προσφορων χρηζει, λεγων οτε μεν, Τι μοι πληθος των θυσιων υμων; λεγει Κυριος. Πληρις ειμι ολοκαυτωματων, και στεαρ αρνων και αιμα ταυρων και τραγων ου βουλομαι⁷. Ουδ' αν ερχησθε οφθηναι μοι, τις γαρ εξεζητησεν ταυτα εκ των χειρων⁸ υμων; Πατειν⁹ μου την αυλην ου προσθησεσθε¹⁰, ουδε εαν φερητε¹¹ σεμιδαλιν ματαιον. Θυμιαμα βδελυγμα μοι εστιν, τας νεομηνιας υμων και τα σαββατα ουκ ανεχομαι.

In MS.:—¹ δικεοσυνη. ² οφιλομεν. ³ υποδιξω. ⁴ οφιλομεν. ⁵ εγκρατια. ⁶ συνευφρενονται. ⁷ βουλομε. ⁸ χιρων. ⁹ πατιν. ¹⁰ προσθησεσθαι. ¹¹ φερηται.

These things, therefore, has He abolished, so that the new law of our Lord Jesus Christ, which is without the yoke of necessity, should have the oblation which is not made by man.

And He again says to them, "Did I at all command your fathers when they came out of the land of Egypt to bring to me burnt offerings and sacrifices? But rather this I commanded them, Let no one of you bear evil malice in his heart against his neighbour, and do not love a false oath."

Then, since we are not without understanding, we ought to perceive the design of our Father's kindness. For he speaks to us, wishing that we, not wandering astray like them [the Jews of old], should seek how we may draw near unto him. To us [Christians] therefore he thus says, 'The sacrifice unto God should be a contrite heart, an odour of sweet smell to the Lord a heart that glorifieth Him that formed it."

Therefore we ought, brethren, to make diligent inquiry about our salvation, so that the Evil one should not by making among us a side entrance of going astray sling us away from our [future] life.

iii.] Therefore He again says to them [the Jews] about these things, "To what end do ye fast unto me as today, saith the Lord, that your voice may be heard by shouting? I chose not such a fast, saith the Lord; not a man afflicting his soul, nor that ye should bow down your neck as a bull-rush, and spread sackcloth and ashes; not thus shall ye call it an acceptable fast."

He says to us, "Behold this is the fast which I have chosen, saith the Lord, not a man afflicting his soul; but loosen thou every bond of injustice, untie the fastenings of

Ταυτα ουν κατηργησεν, ινα ο καινος νομος του Κυριου ημων Ιησου Χριητου, ανευ ζυγου αναγκης ων, μη ανθρωποιητον εχῃ την προσφοραν.

Λεγει δε παλιν προς αυτους, Μη εγω ενετειλαμην[1] τοις πατρασιν υμων εκπορευομενοις εκ γης Λιγυπτου προσενεγκαι μοι ολοκαυτωματα και θυσιας; αλλ' η τουτο ενετειλαμην[1] αυτοις, Έκαστος υμων κατα του πλησιον εν τῃ καρδιᾳ εαυτου κακιαν μη μνησικακειτω[2], και ορκον ψευδη μη αγαπατε[3].

Αισθανεσθαι ουν οφειλομεν[4], μη οντες ασυνετοι, την γνωμην της αγαθωσυνης του Πατρος ημων. Ότι ημιν λεγει θελων ημας μη ομοιως πλανωμενους εκεινοις ζητειν[5] πως προσαγωμεν αυτῳ. Ἡμιν ουν ούτως λεγει, Θυσια τῳ Θεῳ καρδια συντετριμμενη, οσμη ευωδιας τῳ Κυριῳ καρδια δοξαζουσα τον πεπλακοτα αυτην.

Ακριβευεσθαι ουν οφειλομεν[6], αδελφοι, περι της σωτηριας ημων, ινα μη ο πονηρος παρεισδυσιν[7] πλανης ποιησας εν ημιν εκσφενδονησῃ ημας απο της ζωης ημων.

iii.] Λεγει ουν παλιν περι τουτων προς αυτους, Ἱνα τι μοι νηστευετε[8], λεγει Κυριος, ως σημερον ακουσθηναι κραυγῃ την φωνην υμων. Ου ταυτην την νηστιαν εγω εξελεξαμην, λεγει Κυριος, ουκ ανθρωπον ταπεινουντα[9] την ψυχην αυτου, ουδ' αν καμψητε[10] ως κρικον τον τραχηλον υμων, και σακκον και σποδον υποστρωσητε[11], ουδ' ούτως καλεσετε[12] νηστιαν δεκτην.

Προς ημας δε λεγει, Ιδου, αυτη νηστια ην εγω εξελεξαμην, λεγει Κυριος, ουκ ανθρωπον ταπεινουντα[13] την ψυχην αυτου, αλλα λυε παν συνδεσμον αδικιας, διαλυε

In MS. :—[1] ενετιλαμην. [2] μνησικακιτω. [3] αγαπαται. [4] οφιλομεν. [5] ζητιν. [6] οφιλομεν. [7] παρισδυσιν. [8] νηστευεται. [9] ταπινουντα. [10] καμψηται. [11] υποστρωσηται. [12] καλεσεται. [13] ταπινουντα.

violent contracts, send away in freedom the oppressed, and tear asunder every unjust agreement, deal out thy bread to the hungry, and if thou seest a naked man clothe him, bring the roofless into thine own house, and if thou seest a lowly man do not despise him, nor [turn away] from the household of thine own flesh; then shall thy light burst forth early, and thy means of healing will quickly arise, and righteousness will go before thee, and the glory of God will wrap around thee; then thou wilt call out, and God will listen to thee; while thou art yet speaking, he will say, Behold, here I am. If thou shalt put away from thee the yoke, and the pointing with the finger, and the word of muttering, and shalt give to the hungry man thy bread from thy soul, and shalt have pity on the afflicted soul."

To this end therefore, brethren, the long-forbearing [God wrought], having foreseen how the people will believe in sincerity, whom he prepared by means of his Beloved One; for he showed to us beforehand about all things, so that we should not be dashed as proselytes unto their [the Jewish] law.

iv.] Therefore it is right that we, searching out as much as possible about the things which are at hand, should seek for the things which are able to save us. Let us therefore flee altogether from all the works of impiety, lest the works of impiety should take hold of us; and let us hate the error of the present time, so that we may long for the coming time; let us not give a licence to our soul, so that it should have power to run together with sinners and wicked men, lest we should be like them. The final stumblingblock is at hand, about which it is written, as Enoch says, "For unto this end the Almighty has shortened the seasons and the days, so that his Beloved One should hasten, and he will come to his inheritance."

στραγγαλιας βιαιων συναλλαγματων, αποστελλε τεθραυσμενους εν αφεσει, και πασαν αδικον συνγραφην διασπα, διαθρυπτε πεινωσιν¹ τον αρτον σου, και γυμνον εαν ειδης περιβαλε, αστεγους εισαγε εις τον οικον σου, και εαν ιδης ταπεινον² ουχ υπεροψη αυτον, ουδε απο των οικειων³ του σπερματος σου· τοτε ραγησεται προιμον το φως σου, και τα ιαματα σου ταχεως ανατελει, και προπορευσεται εμπροσθεν σου η δικαιοσυνη, και η δοξα του Θεου περιστελει σε, τοτε βοησεις και ο Θεος επακουσεται σου· ετι λαλουντος σου, ερει, Ιδου παρειμι. Εαν αφελης απο σου συνδεσμον, και χειροτονιαν, και ρημα γογγυσμου, και δως πεινωντι⁴ τον αρτον σου εκ ψυχης σου, και ψυχην τεταπεινωμενην⁵ ελεησεις⁶.

Εις τουτο ουν, Αδελφοι, ο μακροθυμος προβλεψας ως εν ακεραιοσυνη⁷ πιστευσει ο λαος ον ητοιμασεν εν τω ηγαπημενω αυτου· προεφανερωσεν γαρ ημιν περι παντων ινα⁸ μη προσρησσωμεθα ως επιλυτοι⁹ τω εκεινων νομων¹⁰.

iv.] Δει ουν ημας περι των ενεστωτων επι πολυ εραυνωντας εκζητειν¹¹ τα δυναμενα ημας σωζειν. Φυγωμεν ουν τελειως απο παντων των εργων της ανομιας, μηποτε καταλαβη ημας τα εργα της ανομιας· και μισησωμεν την πλανην του νυν καιρου, ινα εις τον μελλοντα αγαπηθωμεν· μη δωμεν τη εαυτων ψυχη ανεσιν, ωστε εχειν¹² αυτην εξουσιαν μετα αμαρτωλων και πονηρων συντρεχειν¹³, μηποτε ομοιωθωμεν αυτοις. Το τελειον¹⁴ σκανδαλον ηγγικεν, περι ου γεγραπται ως Ενωχ λεγει. Εις τουτο γαρ ο Δεσποτης συντετμηκεν τους καιρους και τας ημερας, ινα ταχυνη ο ηγαπημενος αυτου, και επι την κληρονομιαν ηξει.

In MS. :—¹ πινωσιν. ² ταπινον. ³ οικιων. ⁴ πινωντι.
⁵ τεταπινωμενην. ⁶ ελαιησεις. ⁷ ακερεοσυνη. ⁸ εινα.
⁹ Conjecture, επηλυτοι. ¹⁰ Conjecture, νομω. ¹¹ εκζητιν. ¹² εχιν.
¹³ συντρεχιν. ¹⁴ τελιον.

And the prophet also says thus, "Ten kingdoms shall reign upon the earth, and after them a little king shall rise up who shall humble three of the kings one after the other." In the same way Daniel says of him, "And I saw the fourth beast, wicked, and strong, and more dangerous above all the beasts of the earth; and there came up as out of it ten horns; and one of them was a little horn, a side sprout; and thus he humbled three of the great horns one after the other."

Ye ought therefore to understand. And I yet also beseech you this, as being one of yourselves and peculiarly so, and loving all above my own soul, to give heed now to yourselves, and not to be like certain persons [the Jews], piling up your sins, and saying, "The Covenant is ours;" whereas they thus lost it for ever, when Moses had only just received it.

For the Scripture says, "And Moses was on the mountain fasting forty days and forty nights, and he received the Covenant from the Lord, the tables of stone written with the finger of the Lord's hand." But they having turned to the idols lost it. For thus says the Lord, "Moses, Moses, go down quickly; for thy people, whom thou broughtest out of the land of Egypt, have acted lawlessly." And Moses perceived, and cast the two tables out of his hands; and their covenant was broken, in order that the covenant of the beloved Jesus might be sealed in our heart in hope of his faith.

And wishing to write many things, (not as a teacher, but as becometh one who loveth,) I hastened to write from [places] which we purpose not to leave. Therefore we notice your defilement in the last days. For all the time of your faith will profit you nothing, unless now in this impious time, and in the coming difficulties, we oppose ourselves as becometh sons of God, so that the Black One should gain no

Λεγει δε ούτως και ο προφητης, Βασιλειαι δεκα επι της γης βασιλευσουσιν, και εξαναστησεται οπισθεν αυτων μικρος βασιλευς ος ταπεινωσει[1] τρεις[2] υφ' εν των βασιλεων. Ομοιως περι αυτου λεγει[3] Δανιηλ, Και ειδον[4] το τεταρτον θηριον πονηρον και ισχυρον και χαλεπωτερον παρα παντα τα θηρια της γης· και ως εξ αυτου ανετειλεν[5] δεκα κερατα, και εξ αυτων μικρον κερας παραφυαδιον· και ως εταπεινωσεν[6] υφ' εν τρια των μεγαλων κερατων. Συνιεναι ουν οφειλετε[7]. Ετι δε και τουτο ερωτω υμας ως εις εξ υμων ων ιδιως[8] δε, και παντας αγαπων υπερ την ψυχην μου, προσεχειν νυν εαυτοις, και μη ομοιουσθαι τισιν επισωρευοντες ταις αμαρτιαις υμων, λεγοντας, ότι η διαθηκη ημων μεν· αλλ' εκεινοι[9] ούτως εις τελος απωλεσαν αυτην, λαβοντος ηδη του Μωυσεως.

Λεγει γαρ η γραφη, Και ην Μωυσης εν τω ορει[10], νηστευων ημερας μ' και νυκτας μ', και ελαβεν την διαθηκην απο του Κυριου, πλακας λιθινας γεγραμμενας τω δακτυλω της χειρος του Κυριου. Αλλα επιστραφεντες επι τα ειδωλα απωλεσαν αυτην. Λεγει γαρ ούτως Κυριος, Μωση, Μωση, καταβηθι το ταχος, ότι ηνομησεν ο λαος σου ους εξηγαγες εκ γης Λιγυπτου. Και συνηκεν Μωσης, και εριψεν τας δυο πλακας εκ των χειρων αυτου· και συνετριβη αυτων η διαθηκη, ίνα η του ηγαπημενου Ιησου ενκατασφραγισθη εις την καρδιαν ημων εν ελπιδι της πιστεως αυτου.

Πολλα δε θελων γραφειν, (ουχ ως διδασκαλος αλλ' ως πρεπει[11] αγαπωντι,) αφ' ων εχομεν μη ελλειπειν[12] γραφειν εσπουδασα. Διο περιψημα υμων προσεχομεν εν ταις εσχαταις ημεραις. Ουδεν γαρ ωφελησει υμας ο πας χρονος της πιστεως υμων, εαν μη νυν εν τω ανομω καιρω, και τοις μελλουσιν σκανδαλοις, ως πρεπει νίοις Θεου

In MS.:—[1] ταπινωσει. [2] τρις. [3] λεγι. [4] ίδον. [5] ανετιλεν. [6] εταπινωσεν. [7] οφιλεται. [8] ίδειως. [9] εκινοι. [10] ορι. [11] πρεπι. [12] ελλιπειν.

side entrance. Let us flee from every vanity. Let us hate thoroughly the works of the wicked way. Do not, while wrapping yourselves in yourselves, live in solitude, as if already justified, but coming together seek for that which is helpful in common. For the Scripture says, "Alas for those who are wise for themselves, and prudent in their own sight." Let us be spiritual, let us be a temple perfect unto God. As much as in us lies let us meditate on the fear of God, so that we may strive to keep his commandments, so that we may rejoice in his acts of justification. The Lord will judge the world without respect of persons; every one as he has done will receive back. If he shall be good, his righteousness will go before him; if he shall be wicked, the reward of his wickedness is in front of him; so that [we should strive] lest while resting at ease, as persons called, we should fall asleep in our sins, and the wicked prince [the Devil], seizing the power over us, should thrust us away from the kingdom of the Lord.

And yet further, my brethren, consider this, when ye see, after such great signs and wonders which had been done in Israel, yet they [the Jews] were thus abandoned; let us take heed lest (as it is written*, "Many are called, but few are chosen") we should be so found.

v.] For unto this end the Lord endured to give up his flesh to corruption, in order that we might be purified by the remission of sins, which comes to pass by the blood of his sprinkling. For it is written about him, partly towards Israel and partly towards us; and it says thus, "He was wounded for our transgressions, and had been weakened for our sins; by his stripes we were healed. He was brought as

---

* Compare Matt. xx. 16 and xxii. 14.

αντιστα μεν ινα μη σχη παρεισδυσιν¹ ὁ μελας. Φυγωμεν απο πασης ματαιοτητος. Μισησωμεν τελειως² τα εργα της πονηριας ὁδου. Μη καθ' ἑαυτους ενδυνοντες μοναζετε³ ὡς ηδη δεδικαιωμενοι· αλλ' επι το αυτο συνερχομενοι συνζητειτε περι του κοινη συμφεροντος. Λεγει γαρ ἡ γραφη, Ουαι οἱ συνετοι ἑαυτοις, και ενωπιον ἑαυτων επιστημονες. Γενωμεθα πνευματικοι, γενωμεθα ναος τελειος⁴ τῳ Θεῳ. Εφ' ὁσον εστιν εν ἡμιν μελετωμεν τον φοβον του Θεου, φυλασσειν⁵ ινα αγωνιζωμεθα τας εντολας αυτου, ινα εν τοις δικαιωμασιν αυτου ευφρανθωμεν. Ὁ Κυριος απροσωπολημπτως κρινει⁶ τον κοσμον, ἑκαστος καθως εποιησεν κομιειται. Εαν ῃ αγαθος, ἡ δικαιοσυνη αυτου προηγησεται αυτου· εαν ῃ πονηρος, ὁ μισθος της πονηριας εμπροσθεν αυτου· ινα μηποτε επαναπαυομενοι, ὡς κλητοι, επικαθυπνωσωμεν ταις ἁμαρτιαις ἡμων, και ὁ πονηρος αρχων λαβων την καθ' ἡμων εξουσιαν απωσηται ἡμας απο της βασιλειας⁷ του Κυριου.

Ετι δε κἀκεινο⁸, Ἀδελφοι μου, νοειτε⁹, οταν βλεπετε¹⁰ μετα τηλικαυτα σημεια¹¹ και τερατα τα γεγονοτα εν τῳ Ισραηλ, και οὑτως ενκαταλελειφθαι¹² αυτους, προσεχωμεν μηποτε (ὡς γεγραπται, Πολλοι κλητοι ολιγοι δε εκλεκτοι) ευρεθωμεν.

v.] Εις τουτο γαρ ὑπεμεινεν¹³ ὁ Κυριος παραδουναι την σαρκα εις καταφθοραν, ινα τῃ αφεσει των ἁμαρτιων ἁγνισθωμεν, ὁ εστιν εν τῳ αἱματι του ραντισματος αυτου. Γεγραπται γαρ περι αυτου, ἁ μεν προς τον Ισραηλ, ἁ δε προς ἡμας· λεγει δε οὑτως, Ετραυματισθη δια τας ανομιας ἡμων, και μεμαλακισται δια τας ἁμαρτιας ἡμων, τῳ μωλωπι αυτου ἡμεις¹⁴ ιαθημεν. Ὡς προβατον επι

In MS.:—¹ πάρισΰυσιν. ² τελιως. ³ μοναζεται. ⁴ τελιος.
⁵ φυλασσιν. ⁶ κριυι. ⁷ βασιλιας. ⁸ κακινο. ⁹ νοειται.
¹⁰ βλεπεται. ¹¹ σημια. ¹² ενκαταλελιφθαι. ¹³ υπεμινεν. ¹⁴ ημις.

a sheep to the slaughter, and was as a lamb dumb before him who sheared it."

Therefore we ought to be very grateful to the Lord, because he made known to us the things that are past, and gave us wisdom in things present, and we are not without understanding as to things which are to come. And the Scripture says, "Not unjustly are nets spread out for birds." It says this because a man perishes justly, who having knowledge of the way of righteousness hurries himself off into the way of darkness.

And yet further, my brethren, if the Lord endured to suffer for our souls, being himself Lord of the whole world, to whom God said, at the foundation of the world*, "Let us make a man after our own image and likeness," how then he endured to suffer under the hand of man, do ye learn. The prophets receiving grace from him prophesied of him. ²And he, in order that he might abolish death, and show forth the resurrection from the dead, (because it was necessary that he should be shown in the flesh,) endured, in order that he should fulfil the promise made to the fathers, and that he while preparing a new people for himself should further show, being himself on the earth, that he who made the resurrection will himself judge them.

And further therefore, when teaching Israel, and doing such great wonders and signs, he preached; and they greatly loved him. And when he chose his own apostles, who were to preach his Good Tidings, he chose those who were neglectors of the Law, [in matters important] above all sin, in order that he might show that he came to call not the righteous but sinners†. Then he showed that he was the

---

* Comp. John, i. 2.　　　　† Comp. Matt. ix. 13.

σφαγην ηχθη, και ως αμνος αφωνος εναντιον του κειραντος¹ αυτον. Ουκουν υπερευχαριστειν² οφειλομεν³ τω Κυριω, οτι και τα παρελελυθοτα ημιν εγνωρισεν, και εν τοις ενεστωσιν ημας εσοφισεν, και εις τα μελλοντα ουκ εσμεν ασυνετοι. Λεγει δε η γραφη, Ουκ αδικως εκτεινεται⁴ δικτυα πτερωτοις. Τουτο λεγει⁵ οτι δικαιως απολειται⁶ ανθρωπος ο εχων οδου δικαιοσυνης γνωσιν εαυτον εις οδον σκοτους αποσυνεχει.

Ετι δε και τουτο, Αδελφοι μου, ει ο Κυριος υπεμεινεν⁷ παθειν περι της ψυχης ημων, ων παντος του κοσμου Κυριος, ω ειπεν ο Θεος απο καταβολης κοσμου, Ποιησωμεν ανθρωπον κατ' εικονα⁸ και καθ' ομοιωσιν ημετεραν· πως ουν υπεμεινεν⁹ υπο χειρος¹⁰ ανθρωπων παθειν μαθετε¹¹. Οι προφηται απ' αυτου εχοντες την χαριν εις αυτον επροφητευσαν. Αυτος δε ινα¹² καταργησει τον θανατον και την εκ νεκρων αναστασιν δειξει (οτι εν σαρκι εδει αυτον φανερωθηναι) υπεμεινεν¹³, ινα και τοις πατρασιν την επαγγελιαν αποδω· και αυτος εαυτω τον λαον τον καινον¹⁴ ετοιμαζων επιδειξει, επι της γης ων, οτι την αναστασιν αυτος ποιησας κρινει¹⁵.

Περας γε τοι διδασκων τον Ισραηλ, και τηλικαυτα τερατα και σημεια¹⁶ ποιων, εκηρυσσεν· και υπερηγαπησαν αυτον. Οτε δε τους ιδιους αποστολους τους μελλοντας κηρυσσειν¹⁷ το ευαγγελιον αυτου εξελεξατο οντας υπερ πασαν αμαρτιαν ανομωτερους, ινα δειξη οτι ουκ ηλθεν καλεσαι δικαιους αλλα αμαρτωλους. Τοτε εφανερωσεν

In MS.:—¹ κιραντος. ² υπερευχαριστιν. ³ οφιλομεν.
⁴ εκτινεται. ⁵ λεγι. ⁶ απολιται. ⁷ υπεμινεν. ⁸ ικονα.
⁹ υπεμινεν. ¹⁰ χιρος. ¹¹ μαθεται. ¹² εινα. ¹³ υπεμινεν.
¹⁴ κενον. ¹⁵ κρινι. ¹⁶ σημια. ¹⁷ κηρυσσιν.

Son of God. For if he came not in the flesh men would not at all have been saved by looking on him. When looking at the sun, which is hereafter not to exist, and is the work of His hands, they are not able to fix their eyes on its rays. Therefore the Son of God came in the flesh that he might bring to a head the sum of the sins upon those who had persecuted his prophets to death.

Therefore to this purpose he endured. For God says of the wounding of his flesh, because it was from them [the Jews], "When they shall smite their own shepherd then the sheep of the flock will be scattered and will perish." And he himself wished thus to suffer; for it was necessary, in order that he should suffer on the wood. For he that prophesies about him says, "Spare my soul from the sword, and fasten my flesh with nails, because the synagogue of wicked doers have risen up against me." And again it says, "Behold, I have given my back to scourges and my cheeks to strokes, and my face I have set as a firm rock."

vi.] When, then, he had executed the command, what says he? "Who is he that contendeth with me, let him stand up against me; or who is he that claims a right of me, let him draw near to the Servant of the Lord." "Alas for you! for ye will all wax old as a garment, and the moth will eat you up." And again the prophet says, when as a mighty stone he was laid for crushing, "Behold, I will lay down for the foundations of Zion a stone, precious, chosen, a corner-stone, honourable."

Then what says he? "And he that believeth on it shall live for ever." Is our hope then on a stone? By no means, but [he meant], When the Lord hath placed his flesh with power. For he says, "And he placed me as a firm rock." And the prophet again says, "The stone which the builders

εαυτον ειναι υιον Θεου. Ει γαρ μη ηλθεν εν σαρκι ουδ' αν πως οι ανθρωποι εσωθησαν βλεποντες αυτον. Ότε τον μελλοντα μη ειναι ήλιον, εργον των χειρων[1] αυτου υπαρχοντα, εμβλεποντες ουκ ισχυουσιν εις τας ακτινας αυτου αντοφθαλμησαι. Ουκουν ο υίος του Θεου εν σαρκι ηλθεν ινα το τελειον[2] των αμαρτιων ανακεφαλαιωση τοις διωξασιν εν θανατω τους προφητας αυτου. Ουκουν εις τουτο υπεμεινεν[3]. Λεγει γαρ ο Θεος την πληγην της σαρκος αυτου, ότι εξ αυτων, Όταν παταξωσιν τον ποιμενα εαυτων, τοτε σκορπισθησεται και απολειται[4] τα προβατα της ποιμνης. Αυτος δε ηθελησεν ούτω παθειν, εδει γαρ, ίνα επι ξυλου παθη. Λεγει γαρ ο προφητευων επ' αυτω, Φεισε μου της ψυχης απο ρομφαιας, και καθηλωσον μου τας σαρκας, ότι συναγωγη πονηρευομενων επανεστησαν μοι. Και παλιν λεγει, Ιδου, τεθεικα μου τον νωτον εις μαστιγας, τας δε σιαγονας[5] μου εις ραπισματα, το δε προσωπον μου εθηκα ως στερεαν πετραν.

vi.] Ότε ουν εποιησεν την εντολην τι λεγει; Τις ο κρινομενος μοι, αντιστητω μοι, η τις ο δικαιουμενος μοι ενγισατω τω παιδι Κυριου. Ουαι υμιν, ότι υμεις[6] παντες ως ιματιον παλαιωθησεσθε[7], και σης καταφαγεται υμας. Και παλιν λεγει ο προφητης, επει[8] ώς λιθος ισχυρος ετεθη εις συντριβην, Ιδου, εμβαλω εις τα θεμελια Σιων λιθον πολυτελη εκλεκτον ακρογωνιαιον[9] εντιμον.

Ειτα τι λεγει; Και ο πιστευων εις αυτον ζησεται εις τον αιωνα. Επι λιθον ουν ημων η ελπις; Μη γενοιτο, αλλ' επει εν ισχυι τεθεικεν την σαρκα αυτου Κυριος. Λεγει γαρ, Και εθηκεν με ως στερεαν πετραν. Λεγει δε παλιν ο προφητης, Λιθον ον απεδοκιμασαν οι οικοδο-

In MS.:—[1] χιρων. [2] τελιον. [3] υπεμινεν. [4] απολιται.
[5] σειαγονας. [6] υμις. [7] παλαιωθησεσθαι. [8] επι. [9] ακρογωνιεον.

rejected is become the head of the corner." And again he says, "This is the great and wonderful day which the Lord hath made." I write to you the more simply that ye may understand. I am the offscouring of your love.

What then again says the prophet? "The synagogue [or assembly] of wicked men surrounded me, they encompassed me as bees the honeycomb; and upon my garment they cast lots." Since, then, he was about to be shown and to suffer in the flesh, his suffering was foreshown. For the prophet says against Israel, "Alas for their soul, because they have counselled an evil counsel against themselves, saying*, Let us bind the Righteous One, because he is displeasing to us."

What says Moses, the other prophet, to them? "Behold, thus saith the Lord God, Enter into the good land, of which the Lord sware to your fathers, to Abraham, Isaac, and Jacob; and inherit ye it, a land flowing with milk and honey. And what says Knowledge [or Gnosticism]? Learn ye. "Hope ye," she says, "on him that is about to be made manifest to you in the flesh, namely Jesus." For Man is earth which suffereth; for from the face of the earth was the figure of Adam made. Why then says it, "Into the good land, the land flowing with milk and honey"? Blessed be our Lord, my Brethren, who has placed in us wisdom and the understanding of his hidden things.

For the prophet says, "Who shall understand the parable of the Lord but he that is wise, and hath understanding, and loveth his Lord?" Since then he has renewed us by the remission of our sins, he has made us after another pattern, so as to have the soul of children, as though indeed he had created us again. For the scripture says of us, as it says to

---

* Comp. Wisdom, ii. 12.

μουντες, ούτος εγενηθη εις κεφαλην γωνιας. Και παλιν λεγει, Αύτη εστιν ή ήμερα ή μεγαλη και θαυμαστη ην εποιησεν ο Κυριος. Άπλουστερον ύμιν γραφω ίνα συνιετε. Εγω περιψημα της αγαπης ύμων. Τι ουν λεγει παλιν ο προφητης; Περιεσχεν με συναγωγη πονηρευομενων, εκυκλωσαν με ώσει[1] μελισσαι κηριον, και επι τον ίματισμον μου εβαλον κληρον. Εν σαρκι ουν αυτου μελλοντος φανερουσθαι και πασχειν, προεφανερωθη το παθος. Λεγει γαρ ο προφητης επι τον Ισραηλ, Ουαι τη ψυχη αυτων, ότι βεβουλευνται βουλην πονηραν καθ' έαυτων, ειποντες, Δησωμεν τον δικαιον ότι δυσχρηστος ήμιν εστιν.

Τι λεγει ο αλλος προφητης Μωσης αυτοις; Ιδου, ταδε λεγει Κυριος ο Θεος, Εισελθετε[2] εις την γην την αγαθην, ήν ωμοσεν Κυριος τοις πατρασιν ύμων τω Αβρααμ και Ισακ και Ιακωβ· και κατακληρονομησατε αυτην, γην ρεουσαν γαλα και μελι. Τι δε λεγει ή Γνωσις; Μαθετε. Ελπισατε[3], φησιν, επι τον εν σαρκι μελλοντα φανερουσθαι ύμιν, Ιησουν. Ανθρωπος γαρ γη εστιν πασχουσα, απο προσωπου γαρ της γης ή πλασις του Αδαμ εγενετο. Τι ουν λεγει, Εις την γην την αγαθην, γην ρεουσαν γαλα και μελι; Ευλογητος ο Κυριος ήμων, Αδελφοι, ο σοφιαν και νουν θεμενος εν ήμιν των κρυφιων αυτου.

Λεγει γαρ ο προφητης, Παραβολην Κυριου τις νοησει, ει μη σοφος και επιστημων και αγαπων τον Κυριον αυτου; Επει[4] ουν ανακαινισας ήμας εν τη αφεσει των άμαρτιων εποιησεν ήμας αλλον τυπον, ώς παιδιων εχειν την ψυχην, ώς αν δη αναπλασσοντος αυτου ήμας. Λεγει γαρ ή γραφη περι ήμων ώς λεγει τω Υίω, Ποιησωμεν

In MS.:—[1] ωσι.   [2] εισελθεται.   [3] ελπισαται.   [4] επι.

the Son, "Let us make the man after our own image, after our own likeness; and let them rule over the beasts of the earth and the fowls of the heavens, and the fishes of the sea."

And the Lord said, when he saw our fair figure, "Increase ye, and multiply, and fill the earth." These things [were said] to the Son. Again, I will show thee how the Lord speaks about us. He made a second fashioning in these last days. And the Lord says, "Behold, I make the last things as the first." Towards this, then, the prophet proclaimed, "Enter ye into the land flowing with milk and honey, and have dominion over it." Behold thou then, we have been refashioned, as it says in another prophet, "Behold, saith the Lord, I will take away from these (that is, from those whom the spirit of the Lord foresaw) their stony hearts, and I will put within them hearts of flesh;" because he was about to be manifested in the flesh, and to dwell among us.

For a holy temple, my Brethren, unto the Lord, is the dwelling-place of our hearts*. For again the Lord says, "And wherewith shall I appear before the Lord my God, and be glorified?" "I will confess to thee in the assembly [or church] of my brethren, and I will sing praise to thee within the assembly of holy ones." We then are those whom he has led into the good land. What then mean the milk and honey? That as the child is kept alive first by honey and then by milk, so therefore we also being kept alive by the faith of the promise and by the word, shall live and rule over the earth. But we said above, "And let them increase, and multiply, and rule over the fishes."

Who then is able to govern the beasts, or the fishes, or

---

* Comp. Eph. ii. 22.

καθ' εικονα και καθ' ομοιωσιν ημων τον ανθρωπον, και αρχετωσαν των θηριων της γης, και των πετεινων του ουρανου, και των ιχθυων της θαλασσης. Και ειπεν Κυριος, ιδων το καλον πλασμα ημων, Αυξανεσθε και πληθυνεσθε και πληρωσατε[1] την γην. Ταυτα προς τον Υιον. Παλιν σοι επιδειξω πως προς ημας λεγει Κυριος. Δευτεραν πλασιν επ' εσχατων εποιησεν. Λεγει δε Κυριος, Ιδου, ποιω τα εσχατα ως τα πρωτα. Εις τουτο ουν εκηρυξεν ο προφητης, Εισελθατε[2] εις γην ρεουσαν γαλα και μελι, και κατακυριευσατε αυτης. Ιδε ουν, ημεις[3] αναπεπλασμεθα, καθως παλιν εν ετερω προφητη λεγει, Ιδου, λεγει Κυριος, εξελω τουτων (τουτεστιν ων προεβλεπεν το πνευμα Κυριου) τας λιθινας καρδιας, και εμβαλω σαρκινας, οτι αυτος εν σαρκι εμελλεν φανερουσθαι, και εν ημιν κατοικειν. Ναος γαρ αγιος, Αδελφοι μου, τω Κυριω το κατοικητηριον ημων της καρδιας. Λεγει γαρ Κυριος παλιν, Και εν τινι οφθησομαι[4] τω Κυριω τω Θεω μου, και δοξασθησομαι; Εξομολογησομαι σοι εν εκκλησια αδελφων μου, και ψαλω σοι αναμεσον εκκλησιας αγιων. Ουκουν ημεις εσμεν ους εισηγαγεν εις την γην την αγαθην. Τι ουν το γαλα και το μελι; Οτι πρωτον το παιδιον[5] μελιτι, ειτα γαλακτι ζωοποιειται· ουτως ουν και ημεις[6] τη πιστει[7] της επαγγελιας και τω λογω ζωοποιουμενοι ζησομεν κατακυριευοντες της γης. Προειρηκαμεν δε επανω, Και αυξανεσθωσαν και πληθυνεσθωσαν και αρχετωσαν των ιχθυων.

Τις ουν ο δυναμενος αρχειν[8] θηριων η ιχθυων η

In MS.:—[1] πληρωσαται.   [2] εισελθαται.   [3] ημις.   [4] οφθησομε.
[5] πεδιον.   [6] ημις.   [7] πιστι.   [8] αρχιν.

the fowls of the heavens? For we ought to perceive that to govern is from authority, so that one should command and rule. If, therefore, this is not so at present, yet he hath promised it to us. When? When we ourselves shall have been made perfect so as to become heirs of the covenant of the Lord.

vii.] Therefore do ye understand, ye children of gladness, that the excellent Lord has foreshown all things to us in order that we should know to whom we should for all things give thanks and praise. If, therefore, the Son of God, being the Lord, has foreshown in order that we should know to whom for all things we should give thanks, and being himself about to judge the living and the dead, he suffered in order that the stroke on him might give us life, let us believe that the Son of God could not suffer except for our sakes. Moreover, when crucified, he had vinegar and gall given to him to drink. Hear how the priests of the temple have shown about this. When the command was written, the Lord ordered that whoever should not keep the fast should be put to death; because he himself also was about to offer up the Vessel of the Spirit [the body of Jesus] as a sacrifice for our sins, in order that the type which took place on Isaac, when he was offered upon the altar, should be completed.

What then says he in the prophet? "And let them eat of the goat which is being offered at the fast for all the sins" (attend carefully), "and let the priests alone eat the inner parts unwashed with vinegar." Wherefore? Because unto me, who am about to offer my flesh for the sins of my new people, ye are about to give for drink gall with vinegar. Eat ye alone while the people are fasting and mourning in sackcloth and ashes, in order that he might show that he ought to suffer many things by them. Attend to what he com-

πετεινων¹ του ουρανου; Λισθανεσθαι γαρ οφειλομεν² οτι το αρχειν εξουσιας εστιν, ινα τις επιταξας κυριευσει. Ει ουν ου γινεται³ τουτο νυν, αρα ημιν ειρηκεν. Ποτε; Όταν και αυτοι τελειωθωμεν⁴ κληρονομοι της διαθηκης Κυριου γενεσθαι.

vii.] Ουκουν νοειτε⁵, τεκνα ευφροσυνης, οτι παντα ο καλος Κυριος προεφανερωσεν ημιν, ινα γνωμεν ω κατα παντα ευχαριστουντες οφειλομεν αινειν⁶. Ει ουν ο Υιος του Θεου, ων Κυριος, προεφανερωσεν ινα γνωμεν ω κατα παντα ευχαριστουντες, και μελλων κρινειν⁷ ζωντας και νεκρους επαθεν ινα η πληγη αυτου ζωοποιησει⁸ ημας, πιστευσωμεν οτι ο Υιος του Θεου ουκ ηδυνατο παθειν, ει μη δι' ημας. Αλλα και σταυρωθεις⁹ εποτιζετο οξει και χολη. Ακουσατε περι τουτου πεφανερωκαν οι ιερεις¹⁰ του ναου. Γεγραμμενης εντολης, ος αν μη νηστευση την νηστειαν¹¹ θανατω εξολεθρευθησεται¹², ενετειλατο¹³ Κυριος, επει¹⁴ και αυτος υπερ των ημετερων αμαρτιων εμελλεν το σκευος του πνευματος προσφερειν¹⁵ θυσιαν· ινα και ο τυπος ο γενομενος επι Ισαακ του προενεχθεντος επι το θυσιαν¹⁶ τελεσθηναι.

Τι ουν λεγει εν τω προφητη; Και φαγετωσαν εκ του τραγου προσφερομενου τη νηστεια¹⁷ υπερ πασων των αμαρτιων, (Προσεχετε¹⁸ ακριβως,) και φαγετωσαν οι ιερεις μονοι παντες το εντερον απλυτον μετα οξους. Προς τι; Επειδη εμε, υπερ αμαρτιων μελλοντα του λαου μου του καινου¹⁹ προσφερειν²⁰ την σαρκαν²¹ μου, μελλετε²² ποτιζειν χολην μετα οξους. Φαγετε²³ υμεις²⁴ μονοι του λαου νηστευοντος και κοπτομενου επι σακκου και σποδου· ινα δειξη²⁵ οτι δει²⁶ αυτον πολλα παθειν υπ' αυτων. Ἀ

In MS.:—¹ πετινων. ² οφιλομεν. ³ γεινεται. ⁴ τελιωθωμεν. ⁵ νοειται. ⁶ αινιν. ⁷ κρινιν. ⁸ ζωοποιησι. ⁹ σταυρωθις. ¹⁰ ιερις. ¹¹ νηστιαν. ¹² εξολεθρευθησετε. ¹³ εντιλατο. ¹⁴ επι. ¹⁵ προσφεριν. ¹⁶ Conj. θυσιαστηριον. ¹⁷ νηστια. ¹⁸ προσεχεται. ¹⁹ κενου. ²⁰ προσφεριν. ²¹ Conj. σαρκα. ²² μελλεται. ²³ φαγεται. ²⁴ υμις. ²⁵ διξη. ²⁶ δι.

manded. "Take two goats goodlooking and alike, and offer them. And let the priest take one for a burnt offering, and one for sins." What should they do with the one? "Accursed," saith he, "is the one," (Attend to how the type of Jesus is shown,) "and all of you spit upon it, and pierce it through, and place the scarlet wool around its head, and thus let it be sent into the desert."

And when it is thus done he who carries the goat leads it into the desert, and takes away the wool, and places it on a shrub, called Rachel, of which we are accustomed to eat the sprouts in the field, when we find them. Thus of the thornbush alone the fruits are sweet. What then is this? Notice the one upon the altar, and the other accursed, and that the accursed one is crowned; because they will hereafter on that day see him having about his body a scarlet robe down to his feet, and they will say, "Is not this he whom we once ourselves crucified, and despised and were spitting on? Truly this is he who then said that he was the Son of God. For how like he is to him!" To this end [it ordered] that the goats should be alike, goodly, equal; so that when they should see him coming they should be struck with the likeness of the goat.

Therefore ye see the goat the type of Jesus who was about to suffer. But why is it that they place the wool in the midst of the thorns? It is placed as a type of Jesus before the church, that should any one wish to take away the scarlet wool, it was needful for him to suffer many things, because the thorn is formidable, and he alone that has been oppressed shall master it. Thus he says, "Those who wish to see me, and to lay hold on my kingdom, must obtain me by being oppressed and by suffering"*.

* Comp. Acts, xiv. 22.

ενετειλατο¹ προσεχετε². Λαβετε δυο τραγους καλους και ομοιους, και προσενεγκατε³. Και λαβετω ο ιερευς τον ένα εις ολοκαυτωμα, τον ενα υπερ αμαρτιων. Τον δε ενα τι ποιησωσιν; Επικαταρατος, φησιν, ο εις· (Προσεχετε πως ο τυπος του Ιησου φανερουται,) και εμπτυσατε⁴ παντες και κατακεντησατε⁵ και περιθετε⁶ το εριον το κοκκινον περι την κεφαλην αυτου, και ούτως εις ερημον βληθητω.

Και όταν γενηται ούτως, αγει ο βασταζων τον τραγον εις την ερημον, και αφαιρει⁷ το εριον, και επιτιθησιν αυτο επι φρυγανον το λεγομενον Ραχηλ, ού και τους βλαστους ειωθαμεν τρωγειν εν τη χωρα ευρισκοντες. Ούτω μονης της ραχους οι καρποι γλυκεις εισιν. Τι ουν τουτο εστιν; Προσεχετε τον μεν ενα επι το θυσιαστηριον, τον δε ενα επικαταρατον, και οτι τον εστεφανωμενον επικαταρατον, επειδη⁸ οψονται αυτον τοτε τη ημερα τον ποδηρη εχοντα τον κοκκινον περι την σαρκα, και ερουσιν, Ουχ ούτος εστιν όν ποτε ημεις⁹ εσταυρωσαμεν και εξουθενησαμεν και εμπτυσαντες; Αληθως ούτος ην ο τοτε λεγων εαυτον Υιον του Θεου ειναι. Πως γαρ ομοιος εκεινω. Εις τουτο ομοιους τους τραγους καλους ισους· ίνα όταν ειδωσιν αυτον τοτε ερχομενον εκπλαγωσιν επι τη ομοιοτητι του τραγου.

Ουκουν ειδετε τον τραγον τον τυπον του μελλοντος πασχειν Ιησου. Τι δε ότι το εριον μεσον των ακανθων τιθεασιν; Τυπος εστιν του Ιησου τη εκκλησια θεμενος, ότι ως εαν θελη το εριον αραι το κοκκινον, εδει αυτον πολλα παθειν¹⁰, δια το ειναι φοβεραν την ακανθαν, και θλιβεντα κυριευσαι αυτου. Ούτω φησιν, Οι θελοντες με ιδειν¹¹, και άψασθαι μου της βασιλειας¹² οφειλουσιν¹³ θλιβεντες και παθοντες λαβειν με.

In MS.:—¹ ενετιλατο. ² προσεχεται. ³ προσενεγκαται. ⁴ εμπτυσαται. ⁵ κατακεντησαται. ⁶ περιθεται. ⁷ αφερι. ⁸ επιδη. ⁹ ημις. ¹⁰ παθιν. ¹¹ ιδιν. ¹² βασιλιας. ¹³ οφιλουσιν.

viii.] And what think ye this type was, that it was enjoined on Israel that the men in whom their sins were perfect should offer a heifer, and should slay it, and burn it; and then that the boys should take away the ashes, and put them in vesels and should bind the scarlet wool around a stick, (See, again, there is the type of the cross,) both the scarlet wool and the hyssop; and that thus the boys should sprinkle the people one by one, that they might be cleansed from their sins? Consider how it is said to you in simplicity.

The calf is Jesus; the men who make the offering are the sinners who brought him to slaughter. Then they are no longer men [making the offering], there is no longer the glory of the sinners. And the boys who sprinkle are those who preach to us the Good Tidings of the remission of sins, and the cleansing of the heart; to whom he gave the authority of the Good Tidings (being twelve, in witness of the tribes, because the tribes of Israel are twelve), that they might preach. And why are there three boys that sprinkle? In witness of Abraham, Isaac, and Jacob, because these men were great with God. And why was the wool upon the stick [or wood]? Because the kingdom of Jesus rests upon wood [or the cross], and because they that put their hope on him will live for ever. And why at the same time the wool and the hyssop? Because in his kingdom the days will be foul and evil; in which we shall be saved, because he who suffers in the flesh will be healed through the foulness of the hyssop. And on this account the things which stand thus are clear to us, but are dark to them [the Jews]; because they heard not the voice of the Lord.

ix.] For he again speaks about our ears, how he circumcised our heart. The Lord says, in the prophet, " By the

viii.] Τινα δε δοκειτε [1] τυπον ειναι, οτι εντεταλται τω Ισραηλ προσφερειν [2] δαμαλιν τους ανδρας εν οις εισιν αμαρτιαι τελειαι [3], και σφαξαντας κατακαιειν· και αιρειν [4] τοτε τα παιδια σποδον, και βαλειν [5] εις αγγη, και περιτιθεναι το εριον το κοκκινον επι ξυλον (Ειδε, παλιν ο τυπος ο του σταυρου,) και το εριον το κοκκινον και το ύσσωπον, και ούτως ραντιζειν τα παιδα καθ' ένα τον λαον, ίνα αγνιζωνται απο των αμαρτιων; Νοειτε [6] πως εν απλοτητι λεγεται υμιν. Ό μοσχος ό Ιησους εστιν· οι προσφεροντες ανδρες αμαρτωλοι οι προσενεγκαντες αυτον επι την σφαγην. Ειτα ουκ ετι ανδρες, ουκ ετι αμαρτωλων ή δοξα. Οι δε ραντιζοντες παιδες οι ευαγγελισαμενοι ημιν την αφεσιν των αμαρτιων, και τον αγνισμον της καρδιας, οίς εδωκεν του ευαγγελιου την εξουσιαν, (ουσιν ιβ', εις μαρτυριον των φυλων, ότι ιβ' φυλαι του Ισραηλ,) εις το κηρυσσειν [7]. Δια τι δε τρεις παιδες οι ραντιζοντες; Εις μαρτύριον Αβρααμ, Ισακ, Ιακωβ, ότι ούτοι μεγαλοι τω Θεω. Ότι δε το εριον επι το ξυλον; Ότι η βασιλεια Ιησου επι ξυλου, και ότι οι ελπιζοντες επ' αυτον ζησονται εις τον αιωνα. Δια τι δε άμα το εριον και το ύσσωπον; Ότι εν τη βασιλεια αυτου ήμεραι εσονται ρυπαραι και πονηραι· εν αίς ήμεις [8] σωθησομεθα, ότι ο αλγων σαρκα δια του ρυπου του ύσσωπου ιαται. Και δια τουτο ούτως γενομενα ημιν μεν εστιν φανερα, εκεινοις δε σκοτεινα [9], ότι ουκ ηκουσαν φωνης Κυριου.

ix.] Λεγει γαρ παλιν περι των ωτιων, πως περιετεμεν ημων την καρδιαν. Λεγει Κυριος εν τω προφητη, Εις

In MS.:—[1] δοκιται. [2] προσφεριν. [3] τελιαι. [4] εριν. [5] βαλιν.
[6] νοειται. [7] κηρυσσιν. [8] ημις. [9] σκοτινα.

hearing of the ear they obeyed me." And again he says, "By hearing those shall hear who are afar off; they shall know what I have done; and be ye circumcised in your hearts, saith the Lord." / And again he says, "Hear, O Israel, for these things saith the Lord thy God; Who is he that wisheth to live for ever, let him by hearing hear the voice of my servant." / And again he says, "Hear, O heavens, and give ear, O earth, for the Lord hath spoken." These things are in witness. And again he says, "Hear the word of the Lord, ye rulers of this people." And again he says, "Hear, O ye children, the voice of one crying in the desert." / Therefore He circumcised our ears, so that we should hear the word, and not only that we should believe, but also that the circumcision, in which they [the Jews] trusted, should be abolished.

For He has declared that circumcision was not of the flesh*; but they transgressed, because an evil angel instructed them. / He says to them, "These things saith the Lord your God, (here I find a command,) Do not sow upon thorns, circumcise yourselves to your God." And why says he, "Circumcise your stubbornness of heart, and be not hard of neck"? Receive again; "Behold, saith the Lord, all the nations have uncircumcision, and this people is uncircumcised in their heart" †.

But thou wilt say, "And indeed the people have been circumcised for a seal." But so also are every Syrian and Arab, and all the priests of the idols. Are those men also part of their [the Jews'] covenant? Moreover the Egyptians also are in circumcision. / Learn ye, then, O children of love, about all things; that Abraham, the first who gave the cir-

---

* Comp. Rom. ii. 28.   † Comp. Rom. ii. 29.

ακοην ωτιου υπηκουσαν μου. Και παλιν λεγει, Ακοη ακουσονται οί πορρωθεν, ά εποιησα γνωσονται· και περιτμηθητε[1], λεγει Κυριος, τας καρδιας υμων. Και παλιν λεγει, Ακουε Ισραηλ, ότι ταδε λεγει Κυριος ό Θεος σου, Τις εστιν ό θελων ζησαι[2] εις τον αιωνα, ακοη ακουσατω της φωνης του παιδος μου. Και παλιν λεγει, Ακουε ουρανε, και ενωτιζου γη, ότι Κυριος ελαλησεν. Ταυτα εις μαρτυριον. Και παλιν λεγει, Ακουσατε λογον Κυριου, αρχοντες του λαου τουτου. Και παλιν λεγει, Ακουσατε, τεκνα, φωνης βοωντος εν τη ερημω. Ουκουν περιετεμεν ήμων τας ακοας ίνα ακουσωμεν λογον, και μη μονον πιστευσωμεν ήμεις[3], αλλα και ή περιτομη εφ' ής πεποιθασιν καταργηται.

Περιτομην γαρ ειρηκεν ου σαρκος γενηθηναι· αλλα παρεβησαν, ότι αγγελος πονηρος εσοφιζεν αυτους. Λεγει προς αυτους, Ταδε λεγει Κυριος ό Θεος υμων, (ώδε εύρισκω εντολην,) Μη σπειρετε[4] επ' ακανθαις, περιτμηθητε[5] τω Θεω υμων. Και τι λεγει περιτμητε[6] την σκληροκαρδιαν υμων, και τον τραχηλον υμων ου σκληρυνειτε; Λαβε παλιν· Ιδου, λεγει Κυριος, παντα τα εθνη ακροβυστιαν, ό δὲ λαος ούτος απεριτμητος καρδιας. Αλλ' ερεις[7], Και μην περιτετμηται ό λαος εις σφραγιδα. Αλλα και πας Συρος και Αραψ και παντες οί ίερεις των ειδωλων[8]. Αρα ουν κάκεινοι εκ της διαθηκης αυτων εισιν; Αλλα και οί Αιγυπτιοι εν περιτομη εισιν. Μαθετε ουν, τεκνα αγαπης, περι παντων· ότι Αβρααμ

In MS. :—[1] περιτμηθηται. [2] ζησε. [3] ημις. [4] σπειρεται. [5] περιτμηθηται. [6] περιτμηται. [7] ερις. [8] ιδωλων.

cumcision, looking forward richly in spirit unto Jesus, practised circumcision, receiving the doctrines of the three letters. For it says, "And Abraham circumcised out of his household eighteen men and three hundred."

What then was the Knowledge given to him? Learn, that it says "eighteen" first, and after making a pause, says "three hundred." Thou hast the eighteen as Jesus; and because the cross in this one was about to have the grace, it says, "and three hundred." It signifies Jesus therefore by the two letters [IH], and by the one [T] the cross. He [Abraham] knew this, because he placed in us the engrafted gift of his covenant. No one has learnt from me a more real word ; but [it is for you] because ye are worthy.

x.] Why did Moses say, "Ye shall not eat the swine, nor the eagle, nor the quick-of-wing, nor the raven, nor a fish which hath not a scale on itself"? He took three doctrines in his mind. Moreover he says in Deuteronomy, "And I will establish my ordinances with this people." Is it not, then, God's command that we should not devour? Moses spoke in spirit. As to the swine, about this he meant, Thou shalt not join thyself, saith he, to such men as are like swine.

That is, when they live riotously they forget the Lord, but when they come to want they remember the Lord; as also the swine while it devours, knows not its master, but when it is hungry it cries out, and on receiving [food] is again silent. "Neither shalt thou eat the eagle, nor the quick-of-wing, nor the kite, nor the raven." Thou shalt not, he means, be joined nor be like to such men, as know not how by labour and sweat to procure the food for themselves, but seize on that of others in their lawlessness, and while walking about in guilelessness are watching, and are looking about for

πρωτος περιτομην δους, εν πνευματι πλουσιως προβλεψας εις τον Ιησουν, περιετεμεν, λαβων γ´ γραμματων δογματα. Λεγει γαρ, Και περιετεμεν Αβρααμ εκ του οικου αυτου ανδρας δεκαοκτω και τριακοσιους. Τις ουν ἡ δοθεισα[1] αυτῳ γνωσις; Μαθετε, ὁτι τους δεκαοκτω πρωτους, και διαστημα ποιησας λεγει τριακοσιους. Το δεκαοκτω εχεις Ιησουν· ὁτι δε ὁ σταυρος εν τουτῳ ημελλεν εχειν[2] την χαριν λεγει, και τριακοσιους. Δηλοι ουν τον μεν Ιησουν εν τοις δυσιν γραμμασιν, και εν τῳ ἑνι τον σταυρον. Οιδεν ὁτι την εμφυτον δωρεαν της διαθηκης αυτου θεμενος εν ἡμιν. Ουδεις γνησιωτερον εμαθεν απ᾽ εμου λογον, αλλα ὁτι αξιοι εστε ὑμεις.

x.] Ὁτι δε Μωσης ειπεν, Ου φαγεσθε χοιρον, ουτε αετον, ουτε οξυπτερον, ουτε κορακα, ουτε ιχθυν ὁς ουκ εχει λεπιδα εν ἑαυτῳ; Τρια ελαβεν εν τῃ συνεσει δογματα. Περας γε τοι λεγει αυτοις εν τῳ Δευτερονομῳ, Και διαθησομαι προς τον λαον τουτον τα δικαιωματα μου. Αρα ουν ουκ εστιν εντολη Θεου το μη τρωγειν; Μωυσης δε εν πνευματι ελαλησεν. Το ουν χοιριον προς τουτο ειπεν, Ου κολληθηση, φησιν, ανθρωποις τοιουτοις, οίτινες εισιν ὁμοιοι χοιρων.

Τουτεστιν, ὁταν σπαταλωσιν επιλανθανονται του Κυριου, ὁταν δε ὑστερουνται επιγινωσκουσιν τον Κυριον· ὡς και ὁ χοιρος ὁταν τρωγει τον κυριον ουκ οιδεν, ὁταν δε πεινα[3] κραυγαζει, και λαβων παλιν σιωπα. Ουτε φαγῃ τον αετον, ουδε τον οξυπτερον, ουδε τον ικτινα, ουτε τον κορακα. Ου μη, φησιν, κολληθησῃ, ουδε ὁμοιωθησῃ ανθρωποις τοιουτοις οίτινες ουκ οιδασιν δια κοπου και ἱδρωτος ἑαυτοις ποριζειν την τροφην, αλλα ἁρπαζουσιν τα αλλοτρια εν ανομιᾳ αυτων, και περιτηρουσιν εν ακεραιοσυνῃ[4] περιπατουντες, και περιβλεπονται τινα εκδυ-

In MS.:—[1] δοθισα. [2] εχιν. [3] πινα. [4] ακερεοσϋνη.

whom they may plunder in covetousness. As also those birds alone do not procure food for themselves by labour; but sitting idle seek how they may eat the flesh of others, being plagues in their wickedness.

"And thou shalt not eat," he says, "the smyrna, nor the polypus, nor the cuttle-fish; they should not eat them." Thou shalt not, he means, be like such men as are ungodly to the end, and are already condemned to death, as those little fishes, which alone are cursed, which swim in the deep, not diving about like the rest, but which dwell in the earth below the deep. / "Moreover thou shalt not eat the hare." Wherefore? Thou shalt not be a corrupter of boys, nor be like to such; because the hare year by year enlarges its place of discharge, for as many years as it lives so many has it. Moreover "Thou shalt not eat the hyena." Thou shalt not be, he means, an adulterer, nor a corrupter, nor be like to such. Wherefore? Because that animal changes its nature every year, and one time is male, and at another time female. Moreover he properly hated the weasel.

Thou shalt not, he means, be such a one as those of whom we hear committing wickedness in the body for uncleanness; nor shalt thou join thyself to women who commit wickedness by the mouth and by uncleanness. For this animal conceiveth in the mouth. / Then about meats, Moses having received three doctrines, thus spoke in spirit : but they after the desire of the flesh received them as about food.

David, however, accepts knowledge of the same three doctrines, and says in like manner, " Blessed is the man who walketh not in the counsel of ungodly," as the fishes go in darkness into the depths; "and who standeth not in the way of sinners," as those who sin while seeming to fear the Lord, as do the swine; "and who sitteth not in the seat of

σωσιν δια την πλεονεξιαν. Ὡς και τα ορνεα ταυτα μονα δια κοπου ἑαυτοις ου ποριζει την τροφην, αλλα αργα καθημενα εκζητει πως αλλοτριας σαρκας φαγῃ, οντα λοιμα τῃ πονηριᾳ αυτων. Και ου φαγῃ, φησιν, σμυρναν ουδε πωλυπαν ουδε σηπιαν, ου μη φαγωσιν. Ου μη, φησιν, ὁμοιωθησῃ ανθρωποις τοιουτοις οἵτινες εισιν ασεβεις εις το τελος, και κεκριμενοι ηδη τῳ θανατῳ, ὡς και ταυτα τα ιχθυδια μονα επικαταρατα τα εν τῳ βυθῳ νηχεται, μη κολυμβωντα ὡς και τα λοιπα, αλλα εν τῃ γῃ κατω του βυθου κατοικει[1]. Αλλα και τον δασυποδα ου μη φαγῃ. Προς τι; Ου μη γενῃ παιδοφθορος, ουδε ὁμοιωθησῃ τοις τοιουτοις· ὅτι ὁ λαγωος κατ' ενιαυτον πλεονεκτει[2] την αφοδευσιν, ὅσα γαρ ετη ζῃ τοσαυτας εχει τρυπας. Αλλ' ουδε την ὑαιναν[3] φαγῃ. Ου μη, φησιν, γενῃ μοιχος, ουδε φθορευς, ουδε ὁμοιωθησῃ τοις τοιουτοις. Προς τι; Ὅτι το ζωον τουτο παρ' ενιαυτον αλλασσει την φυσιν, και τοτε μεν αρρεν, τοτε θηλυ γινεται[4]. Αλλα και την αλην εμισησεν καλως.

Ου μη, φησιν, γενηθῃς τοιουτος οἵους ακουομεν ανομιας ποιουντας εν τῳ σωματι δι' ακαθαρσιαν· ουδε ταις την ανομιαν ποιουσαις εν τῳ στοματι, και ακαθαρσιᾳ κολληθησει. Το γαρ ζωον τουτο τῳ στοματι κυει. Περι μεν των βρωματων λαβων Μωυσης τρια δογματα οὕτως εν πνευματι ελαλησεν, οἱ δε κατ' επιθυμιαν της σαρκος ὡς περι βρωσεως προσεδεξαντο.

Λαμβανει[5] δε των αυτων τριων δογματων γνωσιν Δαυειδ, και λεγει ὁμοιως, Μακαριος ανηρ ὃς ουκ επορευθη εν βουλῃ ασεβων, καθως και οἱ ιχθυες πορευονται εν σκοτει[6] εις τα βαθη· και εν ὁδῳ ἁμαρτωλων ουκ εστη, καθως οἱ δοκουντες φοβεισθαι[7] τον Κυριον ἁμαρτανουσιν, ὡς οἱ χοιροι· και επι καθεδραν λοιμων ουκ εκαθισεν,

In MS.:—[1] κατοικι.   [2] πλεονεκτι.   [3] υεναν.   [4] γεινεται.
[5] λαμβανι.   [6] σκοτι.   [7] φοβισθαι.

the pestilent," as do the birds when sitting for their prey. Hold thou this in a perfect manner. And Moses again says about food, "And eat every thing cloven-footed and that draweth up [the cud.]"

Why says he so? Because when receiving nourishment it knows Him who nourishes it, and resting upon Him it seems to be made glad. He spake well, looking to the commandment. What then does he mean? That we should join ourselves to those who fear the Lord, to those who meditate in their heart on the explanation of the word which they have received, to those who preach the judgments of the Lord and observe them, to those who know that meditation is a work of gladness, and to those who ruminate on the word of the Lord. And why the cloven-footed? Because the just man both walks in this world, and also looks for the holy age. Look how well Moses made his laws. But how could they [the Jews] perceive or understand these things? But we, rightly understanding the commands, rightly preach as the Lord wished. For this purpose he circumcised our ears and hearts, that we might understand these things.

xi.] Let us inquire about this, whether the Lord took care to show beforehand about the water and about the cross. About the water indeed it was written of Israel how they would not receive the baptism which bringeth remission of sins, but would build up one for themselves. For the prophet says, " Be astonished, ye heavens, and let the earth shudder yet more at this, because this people hath done two things, and wicked things; they have forsaken me the fountain of life, and have hewn out for themselves a pit of death. Is my holy hill Sinai a desolate rock? For ye shall be as the young of a bird which fly away when

καθως τα πετεινα¹ καθημενα εις άρπαγην. Εχε τελειως². Και περι της βρωσεως παλιν λεγει Μωυσης, Και φαγεσθε³ παν διχηλουν και μαρυκουμενον. Τι λεγει; Ότι την τροφην λαμβανων οιδεν τον τρεφοντα αυτον, και επ' αυτω αναπαυομενος ευφραινεσθαι⁴ δοκει. Καλως ειπεν βλεπων την εντολην. Τι ουν λεγει; Κολλασθαι μετα των φοβουμενων τον Κυριον, μετα των μελετουντων ὁ ελαβον διασταλμα ρηματος εν τη καρδια, μετα των λαλουντων τα δικαιωματα Κυριου και τηρουντων, μετα των ειδοτων ὅτι ἡ μελιτη εστιν εργον ευφροσυνης, και αναμαρυκωμενον τον λογον του Κυριου. Τι δε το διχηλουν; Ότι και ὁ δικαιος εν τουτω τω κοσμω περιπατει⁵, και τον ἁγιον αιωνα εκδεχεται. Βλεπετε πως ενομοθετησεν Μωυσης καλως. Αλλα ποθεν εκεινοις ταυτα νοησαι η συνιεναι; Ἡμεις δε δικαιως νοησαντες τας εντολας δικαιως λαλουμεν ὡς ηθελησεν ὁ Κυριος. Δια τουτο περιετεμεν τας ακοας ἡμων και τας καρδιας, ἱνα συνιωμεν ταυτα.

xi.] Ζητησωμεν ταυτα, ει εμελησεν τω Κυριω προφανερωσαι περι του ὑδατος και περι του σταυρου. Περι μεν του ὑδατος γεγραπται επι τον Ισραηλ, πως το βαπτισμα το φερον αφεσιν ἁμαρτιων ου μη προσδεξονται, αλλ' ἑαυτοις οικοδομησουσιν. Λεγει γαρ ὁ προφητης, Εκστηθι, ουρανε, και επι τουτω πλειον⁶ φριξατω ἡ γη, ὅτι δυο και πονηρα εποιησεν ὁ λαος οὑτος· εμε εγκατελιπον πηγην ζωης, και ἑαυτοις ωρυξαν βοθρον θανατου. Μη πετρα ερημος εστιν το ορος το ἁγιον μου Σεινα; Εσεσθε⁷ γαρ ὡς πετεινου⁸ νοσσοι ανιπταμενοι νοσσιας αφειρη-

In MS.:—¹ πετινα. ² τελιως. ³ φαγεσθαι. ⁴ ευφρενεσθαι.
⁵ πέριπατι. ⁶ πλιον. ⁷ εσεσθαι. ⁸ πετινου.

removed from the nest." And again the prophet says, "I will go before thee, the mountains I will make level, and the copper gates I will break, and iron bars I will crush, and I will give to thee secret hidden unseen treasures, so that they shall know that I am the Lord God. And thou shalt dwell in a lofty cave of a strong rock, and its water shall be faithful [or unfailing]. Ye shall see a king in glory, and your soul shall meditate on the fear of the Lord."

And again it says in another prophet, "And he who doeth these things shall be as a tree planted by the courses of waters, which shall yield its fruit in its season, and its leaf shall not fall off, and whatever he doeth shall prosper. Not so the ungodly, not so, but may it be as the thistle-down which the wind sweepeth away from the face of the earth. Therefore the ungodly shall not stand up in judgment, nor sinners in the counsel of the righteous; for the Lord knoweth the way of the righteous, and the way of the ungodly shall perish." Mark ye how he has distinguished the water and the cross to the same end. For this means, Blessed are those who while trusting on the cross go down into the water; for their reward, he says, will be in its season; then, says he, I will repay.

And now the [prophet] says "Their leaves shall not fall off." This means that every word which shall go out of your mouth shall be in faith and in love, and for the conversion and hope of many. And again another prophet says, "And indeed the land of Jacob was praised above every land." This means that he will glorify the Vessel of his Spirit [the body of Jesus]. Then what says it? "And there was a river flowing on the right hand; and from it arose beautiful trees; and whoever shall eat of them shall

μενοι. Και παλιν λεγει ο προφητης, Εγω πορευσομαι εμπροσθεν σου, και ορη ομαλιω, και πυλας χαλκας συντριψω, και μοχλους σιδηρους συνκλασω, και δωσω σοι θησαυρους σκοτους, αποκρυφους, αορατους, ινα γνωσιν οτι εγω Κυριος ο Θεος. Και κατοικησεις εν υψηλω σπηλαιω πετρας ισχυρας, και το υδωρ αυτου πιστον· βασιλεα μετα δοξης οψεσθε, και η ψυχη υμων μελετησει φοβον Κυριου.

Και παλιν εν αλλω προφητη λεγει, Και εσται ο ταυτα ποιων ως το ξυλον το πεφυτευμενον παρα τας διεξοδους των υδατων, ο τον καρπον αυτου δωσει εν καιρω αυτου, και το φυλλον αυτου ουκ απορυησεται, και παντα οσα αν ποιη κατευοδωθησεται. Ουχ ουτως οι ασεβεις, ουχ ουτως, αλλ' η ως ο χνους, ον εκριπτει ο ανεμος απο προσωπου της γης. Δια τουτο ουκ αναστησονται οι ασεβεις εν κρισει, ουδε αμαρτωλοι εν βουλη δικαιων· οτι γινωσκει[1] Κυριος οδον δικαιων, και οδος ασεβων απολειται[2]. Αισθανεσθε[3] πως το υδωρ και τον σταυρον επι το αυτο ωρισεν. Τουτο γαρ λεγει[4], Μακαριοι οι επι τον σταυρον ελπισαντες κατεβησαν εις το υδωρ· οτι, Τον μεν μισθον, λεγει, εν καιρω αυτου, τοτε, φησιν, αποδωσω.

Νυν δε ο[5] λεγει, Τα φυλλα ουκ απορυησεται. Τουτο λεγει, οτι παν ρημα ο εαν εξελευσεται εξ υμων δια του στοματος υμων εν πιστει[6] και αγαπη εσται, και επιστροφην και ελπιδα πολλοις. Και παλιν ετερος[7] προφητης λεγει, Και ην η γη του Ιακωβ επαινουμενη παρα πασαν την γην. Τουτο λεγει, το σκευος του πνευματος αυτου δοξασει. Ειτα τι λεγει; Και ην ποταμος ελκων εκ δεξιων, και ανεβαινεν εξ αυτου δενδρα ωραια, και ος αν

In MS. :—[1] γεινωσκι.   [2] απολιται.   [3] αισθανεσθαι.   [4] λεγι.
[5] Conjecture, ο προφητης.   [6] πιστι.   [7] εταιρος.

live for ever"*;/because we indeed go down into the water burdened with sins and filth, and we come up again bearing fruit in the heart, and having the fear [of God] and the trust in Jesus in our spirit. "And whoever shall eat of these will live for ever." This means, Whoever, says he, shall hear these things which are being spoken [or preached], and shall believe, shall live for ever.

xii.] In like manner he again distinguishes about the cross in another prophet, saying, "And at some time these things will come to pass, saith the Lord, when a tree shall be bent down and shall stand up again, and when blood shall drip out of the tree." Thou hast again about the cross, and about him who is to be crucified.

And he again speaks to Moses, when Israel is being defeated under the foreigners. And that he might remind them when being defeated that they were delivered up to death for their sins, the Spirit says to the heart of Moses, that he should make a figure of the cross of him that was to suffer; "for unless," says he, "they put their trust on him they will be defeated for ever." Moses therefore placed one weapon upon another in the middle of the fight, and standing so as to be higher than all, stretched out his hands; and thus Israel again conquered. Then when he let [his hands] down, they were killed. Wherefore? In order that they should know that they cannot be saved unless they put their trust on him [or on the cross].

And again in another prophet he says, "I have all the day stretched forth my hands to a people unbelieving, and contradictory to my just path." ·

Again Moses makes a type of Jesus, that it was necessary

---

* Compare Rev. xxii. 1, 2.

φαγη εξ αυτων ζησεται εις τον αιωνα· ότι ημεις[1] μεν καταβαινομεν[2] εις το ύδωρ γεμοντες αμαρτιων και ρυπου, και αναβαινομεν[3] καρποφορουντες εν τη καρδια, και τον φοβον, και την ελπιδα εις τον Ιησουν εν τω πνευματι εχοντες. Και ός αν φαγη απο τουτων ζησεται εις τον αιωνα. Τουτο λεγει, Ός αν, φησιν, ακουση τουτων λαλουμενων, και πιστευσει, ζησεται εις τον αιωνα.

xii.] Ομοιως παλιν περι του σταυρου οριζει εν αλλω προφητη, λεγων, ότι και ποτε ταυτα συντελεσθησεται, λεγει Κυριος, όταν ξυλον κλιθη και αναστη, και όταν εξ ξυλου αίμα σταξη. Εχεις παλιν περι του σταυρου και του σταυρουσθαι μελλοντος.

Λεγει δε παλιν τω Μωυση, πολεμουμενου του Ισραηλ υπο των αλλοφυλων. Και ίνα υπομνησει αυτους πολεμουμενους, ότι δια τας αμαρτιας αυτων παρεδοθησαν εις θανατον, λεγει εις την καρδιαν Μωσεως το πνευμα, ίνα ποιηση τυπον του σταυρου του μελλοντος πασχειν, ότι εαν μη, φησιν, ελπισωσιν επ' αυτω εις τον αιωνα πολεμηθησονται. Τιθησιν ουν Μωυσης έν εφ' έν όπλον εν μεσω της πυγμης, και υψηλοτερος σταθεις[4] παντων εξετεινεν[5] τας χειρας[6], και ούτως παλιν ενικα ο Ισραηλ. Ειτα όποταν καθειλεν[7] εθανατουντο. Προς τι; Ίνα γνωσιν ότι ου δυνανται σωθηναι εαν μη επ' αυτω ελπισωσιν. Και παλιν εν ετερω προφητη λεγει, Όλην την ημεραν εξεπετασα τας χειρας μου προς λαον απειθη[8], και αντιλεγοντα οδω δικαια μου.

Παλιν Μωσης ποιει τυπον του Ιησου, ότι δει[9] αυτον

In MS.:—[1] ημις. [2] καταβενομεν. [3] αναβενομεν. [4] σταθις.
[5] εξετινεν. [6] χιρας. [7] καθιλεν. [8] απιθη. [9] δι.

for him to suffer, and he will himself make us to live, he who they thought had perished, in the sign of Israel falling. For the Lord made every kind of serpent to bite them, and they died, (since the transgression through the serpent had happened in the case of Eve,) so that he might convince them, that because of their transgression they were given up into the straits of death. / And moreover this man Moses when commanding, "Ye shall not have either a molten image or a graven image for your God," himself wrought that he should show a type of Jesus. Therefore Moses wrought a copper serpent, and placed it in an honourable manner, and called the people by proclamation. / When then they came together they besought Moses that he would offer up prayer for them, for their healing.

And Moses spake to them, "When," saith he, "any one of you shall be bitten let him come to the serpent which is placed on the pole, and let him hope with belief that it though dead is able to give life; and immediately he will be saved"*. And thus they did. Thou hast again in these things the glory of Jesus, for in him and for him are all things†. / What again says Moses to Jesus the son of Naue [Joshua the son of Nun] when he gave to him this name, as being a prophet, that all the people should only hear, and that the Father would make all things known about his son Jesus? / Moses therefore says to Jesus the son of Nave, on giving him this name, when he sent him as a spy of the land, "Take a book in thy hands, and write what the Lord saith, that thou shalt cut off from the roots the whole house of Amalek, thou the son of God, in the

---

* Compare John, iii. 14.   † Col. i. 16.

παθειν, και αυτος ζωοποιησει, ον αν δοξουσιν απολωλεκεναι, εν σημειω¹ πιπτοντος του Ισραηλ. Εποιησεν γαρ Κυριος παντα οφιν δακνειν² αυτους, και απεθνησκον, (επειδη³ η παραβασις δια του οφεως εν Ευα εγενετο,) ινα ελεγξη αυτους οτι δια την παραβασιν αυτων εις θλιψιν θανατου παραδοθησονται. Περας γε τοι ουτος Μωυσης εντειλαμενος⁴, Ουκ εστιν υμιν ουτε χωνευτον ουτε γλυπτον εις Θεον υμιν, αυτος ποιει ινα τυπον του Ιησου δειξει. Ποιει ουν Μωυσης χαλκουν οφιν, και τιθησιν ενδοξως, και κηρυγματι καλει⁵ τον λαον. Ελθοντες ουν επι το αυτο εδεοντο Μωσεως ινα περι αυτων ανενεγκη δεησιν περι της ιασεως αυτων.

Ειπεν δε Μωσης προς αυτους, Οταν, φησιν, δηχθη τις υμων, ελθετω επι τον οφιν τον επι του ξυλου επικειμενον, και ελπισατο πιστευσας οτι αυτος ων νεκρος δυναται ζωοποιησαι· και παραχρημα σωθησεται. Και ουτως εποιουν. Εχεις παλιν και εν τουτοις την δοξαν του Ιησου, οτι εν αυτω τα παντα και εις αυτον. Τι λεγει παλιν Μωυσης Ιησου υιω Ναυη επιθεις αυτω τουτο το ονομα, οντι προφητη, ινα μονον ακουση πας ο λαος, οτι ο Πατηρ παντα φανεροι περι του Υιου Ιησου; Λεγει ουν Μωυσης Ιησου υιω Ναυη επιθεις τουτο ονομα οποτε επεμπεν αυτον κατασκοπον της γης, Λαβε βιβλιον εις τας χειρας⁶ σου, και γραψον ά λεγει Κυριος, οτι εκκοψεις εκ ριζων τον οικον παντα του Αμαληκ ο υιος του Θεου επ'

In MS.—¹ σημιω. ² δακνιν. ³ επιδη. ⁴ εντιλαμενος. ⁵ καλι.
⁶ χιρας.

last days." Behold again, Jesus was not the son of man, but the son of God, and was by a figure made manifest in flesh*.

Since then they were to say that Christ was the son of David, David himself, fearing and understanding the error of the sinful, prophesied, "The Lord said to my lord, Sit thou on my right hand until I make thine enemies a footstool for thy feet"†. And again thus says Isaiah, "The Lord said to Cyrus, mine anointed one, whose right hand he held, Nations shall yield obedience before him, and I will break in pieces the strength of kings." Behold how David calls him Lord and the son of God.

xiii.] And let us see whether this people or the former is the heir, and whether the covenant is for us or for them. Hear then about the people, what the scripture says. "And Isaac prayed for Rebecca his wife because she was barren; and she conceived." "Then Rebecca went to inquire from the Lord, and the Lord said to her 'Two nations are in thy womb, and two peoples in thy belly, and one people shall be more powerful than the other people, and the greater [or elder] shall serve the smaller [or younger].'"

You ought to understand who Isaac was, and who Rebecca, and about whom he has shown that this people should be greater than that. And in another prophecy Jacob says yet more clearly to Joseph his son, saying, "Behold, the Lord hath not deprived me of thy presence; bring thy sons to me that I may bless them." And he brought Ephraim and Manasseh, wishing that he should bless Ephraim [this should be Manasseh], as he was the elder. For Joseph brought [him] to the right hand of his father Jacob. And

* 1 Tim. iii. 16.   † Matt. xxii. 44.

εσχατων των ημερων. Ειδε παλιν, Ιησους, ουχι υιος ανθρωπου, αλλα υιος του Θεου, τυπω δε εν σαρκι φανερωθεις.

Επει¹ ουν μελλουσιν λεγειν οτι Χριστος υιος Δαβιδ εστιν, αυτος προφητευει Δαβιδ φοβουμενος και συνιων την πλανην των αμαρτωλων, Ειπεν Κυριος τω κυριω μου, καθου εκ δεξιων μου εως αν θω τους εχθρους σου υποποδιον των ποδων σου. Και παλιν λεγει ουτως Ησαιας, Ειπεν Κυριος τω χριστω μου Κυρω ου εκρατησεν της χειρος της δεξιας αυτου, επακουσαι² εμπροσθεν αυτου εθνη, και ισχυν βασιλεων διαρρηξω. Ειδε πως Δαβιδ λεγει αυτον Κυριον και υιον Θεου.

xiii.] Ειδωμεν δε ει ουτος ο λαος κληρονομει ει ο πρωτος, και η διαθηκη εις ημας η εις εκεινους. Ακουσατε ουν περι του λαου, τι λεγει η γραφη. Εδειτο δε Ισαακ περι Ρεβεκκας της γυναικος αυτου, οτι στειρα³ ην· και συνελαβεν. Ειτα εξηλθεν Ρεβεκκα πυθεσθαι παρα Κυριου, και ειπεν Κυριος προς αυτην, Δυο εθνη εν τη γαστρι σου, και δυο λαοι εν τη κοιλια σου, και υπερεξει λαος λαου, και ο μειζον⁴ δουλευσει τω ελασσονι.

Αισθανεσθαι οφειλετε⁵ τις ο Ισαακ, και τις η Ρεβεκκα, και επι τινων δεδειχεν⁶ οτι μειζων ο λαος ουτος η εκεινος. Και εν αλλη προφητεια⁷ λεγει φανερωτερον ο Ιακωβ προς Ιωσηφ τον υιον αυτου, λεγων, Ιδου, ουκ εστερησεν με Κυριος του προσωπου σου· προσαγαγε μοι τους υιους σου, ινα ευλογησω αυτους. Και προσηγαγεν Εφραιμ και Μανασση, θελων τον Εφραιμ ινα ευλογηση, οτι πρεσβυτερος ην. Ο γαρ Ιωσηφ προσηγαγεν εις την δεξιαν χειρα του πατρος Ιακωβ. Ειδεν δε Ιακωβ τυπον

In MS.:—¹ επι.   ² επακουπε.   ³ στιρα.   ⁴ Conj. μειζων.
⁵ οφιλεται.   ⁶ ϊεϊιχεν.   ⁷ προφητια.

Jacob saw in spirit the type of the future people. And what does it say? "And Jacob set his hands crosswise, and placed his right hand on the head of Manasseh [this should be Ephraim], the second and younger, and blessed him. And Joseph said to Jacob, Change thy right hand on to the head of Ephraim [this should be Manasseh]; for he is my first born son. And Jacob said to Joseph, I know it, my child, I know it, but the elder shall serve the younger; and he also shall be blessed."

Ye see upon which of them it was fit, that this people should be first and heir of the covenant. If then moreover through Abraham it was mentioned, we have the full perfection of our knowledge. What then says it to Abraham, when he alone on believing was placed in righteousness? "Behold, I have made thee, Abraham, the father of the nations which believe in God though in uncircumcision"*.

xiv.] Yes, but let us know whether the covenant which he swore that he would give to the fathers, to give to the people, whether he has given it. He has given it, but they were not worthy to receive it because of their sins. For the prophet says, "And Moses was fasting forty days and 40 nights on Mount Sinai that he might receive the covenant of the Lord for the people." And Moses received from the Lord the two tables written in spirit with the finger of the Lord's hand. And Moses when he received them brought them down to give them to the people.

And the Lord said to Moses, "Moses, Moses, go down quickly, because thy people, whom thou broughtest out from the land of Egypt, hath broken the law." And Moses perceived that they had made for themselves molten images;

* Comp. Rom. iv. 3.

τω πνευματι του λαου του μεταξυ. Και τι λεγει; Και εποιησεν Ιακωβ εναλλαξας τας χειρας [1] αυτου, και επεθηκεν την δεξιαν επι την κεφαλην Μανασση του δευτερου και νεωτερου, και ευλογησεν αυτον. Και ειπεν Ιωσηφ προς Ιακωβ, Μεταθες σου την δεξιαν επι την κεφαλην Εφραιμ, ότι πρωτοτοκος μου υίος εστιν. Και ειπεν Ιακωβ προς Ιακωβ [2], Οιδα, τεκνον, οιδα, αλλ' ό μειζων [3] δουλευσει τω ελασσονι· και ούτος δε ευλογηθησεται. Βλεπετε επι τινων εοικεν, τον λαον τουτον ειναι πρωτον και της διαθηκης κληρονομον. Ει ουν ετι και δια του Λβρααμ εμνησθη, απεχομεν το τελειον [4] της γνωσεως ήμων. Τι ουν λεγει τω Λβρααμ ότε μονος πιστευσας ετεθη εις δικαιοσυνην; Ιδου, τεθεικα [5] σε Λβρααμ πατερα εθνων των πιστευοντων δι' ακροβυστιαν τω Θεω.

xiv.] Ναι, αλλα ειδωμεν ει ή διαθηκη, ήν ωμοσεν δουναι τοις πατρασιν δουναι τω λαω, ει δεδωκεν. Δεδωκεν, αυτοι δε ουκ εγενοντο αξιοι λαβειν δια τας ὑμαρτιας αυτων. Λεγει γαρ ό προφητης, Και ην Μωυσης νηστευων εν όρει [6] Σινα του λαβειν την διαθηκην Κυριου προς τον λαον ἡμερας τεσσαρακοντα και νυκτας μ'. Και ελαβεν Μωσης παρα Κυριου τας δυο πλακας τας γεγραμμενας τω δακτυλω της χειρος Κυριου εν πνευματι. Και λαβων Μωσης κατεφερεν προς τον λαον δουναι.

Και ειπεν Κυριος προς Μωσην, Μωση Μωση, καταβηθι το ταχος, ότι ό λαος σου όν εξηγαγες εκ γης Αιγυπτου ηνομησεν. Και συνηκεν Μωσης ότι εποιησαν ἑαυτοις χωνευματα· και ερριψεν [7] εκ των χειρων [8] τας πλακας, και

In MS.:—[1] χιρας.   [2] Conj. Ιωσηφ.   [3] μιζων.   [4] τελιον
[6] ορι.   [7] ερρειψεν.   [8] χιρων.

and he threw the tables out of his hands, and the tables of the Lord's covenant were broken to pieces. 'Moses indeed had received it; but they were not worthy. And how we received it, learn ye. Moses received it as being a servant*; but the Lord himself gave it to us, that we might be the people of inheritance, since he had waited for us. And he was manifested, so that those [the Jews] should be made perfect in their sins, and that we, through the Lord Jesus, who made us heirs, should receive the covenant of Christ; who was prepared to this end, that he when appearing, redeeming from darkness our hearts which had been already wasted unto death, and had been given up to the sinfulness of error, should establish in us the covenant by his word. For it is written how the Father commanded him that redeeming us from darkness he should prepare us a holy people for himself.

Therefore the prophet says "I the Lord thy God have called thee in righteousness, and I will hold thy hand, and will strengthen thee; and I have given thee to be a covenant for the people, to be a light for the nations, to open the eyes of the blind, and to lead forth from fetters those who have been bound, and out of the prison-house those that are sitting in darkness." Therefore we know whence we have been redeemed. Again the prophet says, "The Spirit of the Lord is upon me, because he has anointed me to preach good tidings to the poor; he has sent me to heal the brokenhearted, to preach deliverance to the captives, and recovery of sight to the blind, to proclaim the acceptable year of the the Lord, and the day of recompense, to comfort all that mourn." Again the prophet says, "Behold, I have set thee

---

* Heb. iii. 5.

συνετριβησαν αἱ πλακες της διαθηκης Κυριου. Μωσης μεν ελαβεν, αυτοι δε ουκ εγενοντο αξιοι. Πως δε ημεις[1] ελαβομεν μαθετε. Μωσης θεραπων ων ελαβεν, αυτος δε Κυριος ημιν εδωκεν, εις λαον κληρονομιας δι' ημας υπομεινας[2]. Εφανερωθη δε ινα κἀκεινοι[3] τελειωθωσιν[4] τοις ἁμαρτημασιν, και ημεις[5] δια του κληρονομουντος Κυριου Ιησου διαθηκην Χριστου λαβωμεν, ὁς εις τουτο ητοιμασθη, ινα αυτος φανεις[6], τας ηδη δεδαπανημενας ημων καρδιας τῳ θανατῳ, και παραδεδομενας τῃ της πλανης ανομιᾳ, λυτρωσαμενος εκ του σκοτους, διαθηται εν ημιν διαθηκην λογῳ. Γεργαπται γαρ, πως αυτῳ ὁ Πατηρ εντελλεται λυτρωσαμενον ημας εκ του σκοτους ἑαυτῳ ητοιμασε[7] λαον ἁγιον.

Λεγει ουν ὁ προφητης, Εγω Κυριος ὁ Θεος σου εκαλεσα σε εν δικαιοσυνῃ και κρατησω της χειρος[8] σου, και ισχυσω σε, και εδωκα σε εις διαθηκην γενους, εις φως εθνων, ανοιξαι[9] οφθαλμους τυφλων, και εξαγαγειν εκ δεσμων πεπεδημενους, και εξ οικου φυλακης καθημενους εν σκοτει[10]. Γινωσκομεν ουν ποθεν ελυτρωθημεν. Παλιν ὁ προφητης λεγει, Πνευμα Κυριου επ' εμε οὐ είνεκεν εχρισεν με ευαγγελισασθαι πτωχοις, απεσταλκεν με ιασασθαι τους συντετριμμενους την καρδιαν, κηρυξαι αιχμαλωτοις αφεσιν, και τυφλοις αναβλεψιν, καλεσαι[11] ενιαυτον Κυριου δεκτον, και ημεραν ανταποδοσεως, παρακαλεσαι[12] παντας τους πενθουντας. Παλιν ὁ προφητης λεγει, Ιδου, τεθεικα σε εις φως εθνων, του

In MS.:—[1] ημις. [2] υπομινας. [3] κακινοι. [4] τελιωθωσιν.
[5] ημις. [6] φανις. [7] Conj. ἑτοιμασαι. [8] χιρος. [9] ανοιξε. [10] σκοτι.
[11] καλεσε. [12] παρακαλεσε.

for a light to the nations, that thou shouldest be for salvation unto the ends of the earth. Thus saith the Lord who redeemeth thee, the God of Israel."

xv.] Moreover it is written about the Sabbath in the Ten Words [or Commandments], which He spoke to Moses face to face on Mount Sinai, "And keep ye holy the sabbath of the Lord, with clean hands and a clean heart." / And in another place he says, "If Israel my sons keep the sabbath, then I will place my mercy upon them." / The sabbath it speaks of in the beginning of the creation [saying], "And God made in six days the works of his hands, and finished on the seventh day, and made it a rest, and made it holy." Notice, my children, what he says, "He finished in six days." This means that in six thousand years the Lord will finish all things; for with him the day means a thousand years; for David witnesses to me saying, that "a thousand years in thine eyes are as yesterday which is past, and as a watch in the night."

And he himself witnesses to me, saying, "Behold, a day of the Lord shall be as a thousand years." Therefore, my children, in six days, that is, in the six thousand years, all things will be finished. / "And he rested on the seventh day." This means, when his Son on coming shall destroy the time, and shall judge the ungodly, and shall change the sun and the stars and the moon*, then he will truly rest on the seventh day. / Moreover he says, "Thou shalt keep it holy with clean hands and a clean heart."

If then any one is now able to keep holy the day which God made holy, otherwise than by being clean of heart in all things, we are deceived. / And if, therefore, on resting properly,

---

* Comp. Rev. vi. 12-17.

ειναι σε εις σωτηριαν έως εσχατου της γης. Ούτως λεγει Κυριος ο λυτρωσαμενος σε, Θεος Ισραηλ.

XV.] Ετι ουν και περι του σαββατου γεγραπται εν τοις δεκα λογοις, εν οίς ελαλησεν εν τω ορει [1] Σινα προς Μωσην κατα προσωπον, Και άγιασατε [2] το σαββατον Κυριου χερσιν καθαραις και καρδια καθαρα. Και εν έτερω [3] λεγει, Εαν φυλαξωσιν οι υίοι μου Ισραηλ το σαββατον, τοτε επιθησω το ελεος μου επ' αυτους. Το σαββατον λεγει εν αρχη της κτισεως, Και εποιησεν ο Θεος εν έξ ήμεραις τα εργα των χειρων [4] αυτου, και συνετελεσεν τη ήμερα τη έβδομη, και κατεπαυσεν αυτην, και ήγιασεν αυτην. Προσεχετε, τεκνα, τι λεγει, το συνετελεσεν εν έξ ήμεραις. Τουτο λεγει ότι εν έξακισχιλιοις ετεσιν συντελεσει [5] Κυριος τα συνπαντα· ή γαρ ήμερα παρ' αυτω σημαινει [6] χιλια ετη· μαρτυρει γαρ μοι Δαβιδ λεγων, ότι χιλια ετη εν οφθαλμοις σου ώς ή ημερα ή εχθες ήτις διηλθεν, και φυλακη εν νυκτι. Αυτος δε μοι μαρτυρει [7] λεγων, Ιδου, ήμερα Κυριου εσται ώς χιλια ετη. Ουκουν, τεκνα, εν έξ ήμεραις, εν τοις έξακισχιλιοις ετεσιν, συντελεσθησεται τα συνπαντα. Και κατεπαυσεν τη ήμερα τη εζ'. Τουτο λεγει, όταν ελθων ο υίος αυτου καταργησει τον καιρον, και κρινει [8] τους ασεβεις, και αλλαξει τον ήλιον και τους αστερας και την σεληνην, τοτε καλως καταπαυσεται τη ήμερα τη έβδομη. Περας γε τοι λεγει, 'Αγιασεις αυτην χερσιν καθαραις και καρδια καθαρα.

Ει ουν, ήν ο Θεος ήμεραν ήγιασεν νυν τις δυναται άγιασαι, ει μη καθαρος ων τη καρδια εν πασιν, πεπλανημεθα. Ει δε ουν, αρα τοτε καλως καταπαυομενοι άγια-

In MS.:— [1] ορι. [2] αγιασαται. [3] εταιρω. [4] χιρων. [5] συντελεσι. [6] σημαινι. [7] μαρτυρι. [8] κρινι.

E

then we shall keep it holy, when we ourselves shall be able, after having been justified, and having received the promise, when there is no longer any wickedness, and all things have been made new by the Lord,—then we shall be able to keep it holy, when we ourselves have first been made holy. Moreover he says to them, "Your new moons and your sabbaths I cannot bear."

Ye see how he says, "Your present sabbaths are not acceptable; but that [sabbath] which I have made, in which, when having made all things rest, I shall make the beginning of the eighth day," that is, the beginning of another world. Therefore let us also keep the eighth day in joyfulness, in which also our Lord Jesus the Christ rose from the dead, and when he had been made manifest went up to heaven.

xvi.] Moreover about the temple I will tell you how the wretched people [the Jews] wandering, put their hope on the building, and not upon their God who made them, considering it the House of God. For almost after the manner of the Gentiles they hallowed Him in [hallowing] the temple. But how the Lord speaks, when abolishing it, learn ye: "Who measured out the heavens with a span, and the earth with a hand-breadth? Was it not I? saith the Lord. The heavens are my throne, and the earth is a footstool for my feet: what house will ye build for me, or which is the place of my rest?"

Ye know that their [the Jews'] hope is vain. Moreover t again says, "Behold they who destroyed this temple, shall themselves build it up." For because of their going to war it was destroyed by the enemies, and now they and the servants of the enemies shall rebuild it. Again, it was made plain how the city and the people and the temple of Israel were delivered up. For the Scripture says, "And it shall

σομεν αυτην, οτε δυνησομεθα αυτοι δικαιωθεντες και απολαβοντες την επαγγελιαν, μηκετι ουσης της ανομιας, καινων δε γεγονοτων παντων υπο του Κυριου,—τοτε δυνησομεθα αυτην αγιασαι[1] αυτοι αγιασθεντες πρωτον. Περας γε τοι λεγει αυτοις, Τας νεομηνιας υμων και τα σαββατα ουκ ανεχομαι.

Ορατε[2] πως λεγει, Ου τα νυν σαββατα δεκτα, αλλ' ο πεποιηκα, εν ω, καταπαυσας τα παντα, αρχην ημερας ογδοης ποιησω, ο εστιν, αλλου κοσμου αρχην. Διο και αγομεν την ημεραν την ογδοην εις ευφροσυνην, εν η και ο Κυριος ημων Ιησους ο Χριστος ανεστη εκ νεκρων, και φανερωθεις ανεβη εις ουρανους.

xvi.] Ετι δε και περι του ναου ερω υμιν ως πλανωμενοι οι ταλαιπωροι εις την οικοδομην ηλπισαν, και ουκ επι τον Θεον αυτων τον ποιησαντα αυτους, ως οντα οικον Θεου. Σχεδον εις τα εθνη αφιερωσαν γαρ αυτον εν τῳ ναῳ. Αλλα πως λεγει Κυριος καταργων αυτον, μαθετε[3]· Τις εμετρησεν τον ουρανον σπιθαμῃ, η την γην δρακι[4]; Ουκ εγω; λεγει Κυριος. Ο ουρονος μοι θρονος, η δε γη υποποδιον των ποδων μου, ποιον οικον οικοδομησετε[5] μοι, η τις τοπος της καταπαυσεως μου; Εγνωκατε[6] οτι ματαια η ελπις αυτων. Περας γε τοι παλιν λεγει, Ιδου, οι καθελοντες τον ναον τουτον αυτοι οικοδομησουσιν αυτον. Δια γαρ το πολεμειν[7] αυτους καθηρεθη υπο των εχθρων, νυν και αυτοι και οι των εχθρων υπηρεται ανοικοδομησωσιν αυτον. Παλιν, ως εμελλεν η πολις και ο λαος και ο ναος Ισραηλ παραδιδοσθαι εφανερωθη. Λεγει γαρ η γραφη, Και εσται επ'

In MS.:—[1] αγιασε. [2] οραται. [3] μαθεται. [4] δρακει. [5] οικοδομησεται. [6] εγνωκαται. [7] πολεμιν.

come to pass in the last days that the Lord will deliver up the sheep of his pasture, and their sheepfold and tower, to destruction." And it happened as the Lord had spoken. And let us seek if there be a temple of God. There is, where he himself says that he will make it and fit it up again. For it is written, "And it shall come to pass when the week is ended, that the temple of God shall be built up gloriously in the name of the Lord." / I find therefore that there is a temple.

How then shall it be built in the name of the Lord? Learn. Before ye believed in our God the dwelling-place of your heart was corrupt and weak, as a temple indeed built by hand. For it was full of idolatry, and was a house of demons through doing such things as were opposed to God. / But it will be built up in the name of the Lord, (and notice,) so that the temple of God shall be built up gloriously. How? Learn. Having received the forgiveness of sins, and hoping in the name of the Lord, we are become new, being again created from the beginning. Therefore in our dwelling-place God indeed dwells within us. How?

His word of faith, the calling according to the promise, the wisdom of the statutes, the commands of the teaching, he himself prophesying within us, he himself dwelling within us, opening to us, who were enslaved to death, the door of the temple, that is, the mouth [of the preacher]; by giving to us repentance, he leads us into the incorruptible temple. For he who wishes to be saved looks not to the man [the preacher], but to Him who dwells within him, and who speaks by him; being amazed at never having either heard Him speaking out of his mouth the words, nor having himself desired to hear. This is the spiritual temple built up for the Lord.

εσχατων των ημερων, και παραδωσει Κυριος τα προβατα της νομης, και την μανδραν και τον πυργον αυτων, εις καταφθοραν. Και εγενετο καθ' ά ελαλησεν Κυριος. Ζητησωμεν δε ει εστιν ναος Θεου. Εστιν, όπου αυτος λεγει ποιειν και καταρτιζειν. Γεγραπται γαρ, Και εσται, της έβδομαδος συντελουμενης, οικοδομηθησεται ναος Θεου ενδοξως επι τω ονοματι Κυριου. Εύρισκω ουν ότι εστιν ναος.

Πως ουν οικοδομηθησεται επι τω ονοματι Κυριου; Μαθετε[1]. Προ του ύμας πιστευσαι τω Θεω ημων το κατοικητηριον της καρδιας φθαρτον και ασθενες, ως αληθως οικοδομητος ναος δια χειρος[2]. Ότι ην πληρεις[3] μεν ειδωλολατρειας[4], και ην οικος δαιμονιων δια το ποιειν όσα ην εναντια τω Θεω. Οικοδομηθησεται δε επι τω ονοματι Κυριου, (προσεχετε δε,) ίνα ό ναος του Θεου ενδοξως οικοδομηθη. Πως; Μαθετε. Λαβοντες την αφεσιν των άμαρτιων, και ελπισαντες επι το ονομα Κυριου, εγενομεθα καινοι[5], παλιν εξ αρχης κτιζομενοι. Διο εν τω κατοικητηριω ημων αληθως ό Θεος κατοικει εν ημιν. Οπως;

Ο λογος αυτου της πιστεως, ή κλησις της επαγγελιας, ή σοφια των δικαιωματων, αί εντολαι της διδαχης, αυτος εν ημιν προφητευων, αυτος εν ημιν κατοικων, τοις τω θανατω δεδουλωμενοις ανυγων[6] ημιν την θυραν του ναου, ό εστιν στομα· μετανοιαν διδους ημιν, εισαγει εις τον αφθαρτον ναον. Ό γαρ ποθων σωθηναι βλεπει ουκ εις τον ανθρωπον, αλλα εις τον εν αυτω κατοικουντα, και λαλουντα επ' αυτω, εκπλησσομενος επι τω μηδεποτε, μητε του λεγοντος τα ρήματα ακηκοεναι εκ του στοματος, μητε αυτος ποτε επιτεθυμηκεναι ακουειν. Τουτ' εστιν πνευματικος ναος οικοδομουμενος τω Κυριω.

In MS.:—[1] μαθεται. [2] χιρος. [3] πληρις. [4] ειδωλολατριας. [5] κενοι. [6] Conj. ανοιγων.

xvii.] As far as it was possible to explain to you in simplicity, my mind and my soul earnestly hope that nothing has been omitted of the things which bear upon salvation. For if I should write to you about things which are beginning, or those which are future, ye will not understand, because such things are hid in parables. These things then are thus.

xviii.] Let us pass on to another kind of knowledge and teaching. There are two ways [or paths] of teaching and authority, the one of light and the other of darkness. And there is much difference between the two ways. For over the one are stationed the light-bringing angels of God, and over the other men are the angels of Satan*. And He is Lord from ages to ages; but he [Satan] is prince of the present time of wickedness.

xix.] The way of light then is this. If any one wishes to travel the way to the appointed place he should press forward by his works. The knowledge then that is given us for walking in this way is the following. Thou shalt love Him that made thee; thou shalt fear Him that formed thee; thou shalt glorify Him that redeemed thee from death. Thou shalt be simple in heart, and rich in spirit. Thou shalt not join thyself to those who walk in the way of death.

Thou shalt hate every thing which is not pleasing to God; thou shalt hate all hypocrisy. Thou shalt not forsake the commandments of the Lord. Thou shalt not exalt thyself, but thou shalt be lowly-minded in all things. Thou shalt not contrive glory for thyself. Thou shalt not take evil counsel against thy neighbour. Thou shalt not give over-boldness to thy soul. Thou shalt not commit fornication; thou shalt not commit adultery; thou shalt not corrupt

---

* 2 Cor. xii. 7.

xvii.] Εφ' όσον ην εν δυνατω και απλοτητι δηλωσαι[1] υμιν ελπιζει μου ο νους και η ψυχη τη επιθυμια μου μη παραλελοιπεναι[2] τι των ανηκοντων εις σωτηριαν. Εαν γαρ περι των ενεστωτων η μελλοντων γραψω υμιν ου μη νοησητε[3], δια το εν παραβολαις κεισθαι[4]. Ταυτα μεν ούτως.

xviii.] Μεταβωμεν γε εφ' ετεραν γνωσιν και διδαχην. Όδοι δυο εισιν διδαχης και εξουσιας, η του φωτος και η του σκοτους. Διαφορα δε πολλη των δυο οδων. Εφ' ης μεν γαρ εισιν τεταγμενοι φωταγωγοι αγγελοι του Θεου, εφ' οις δε αγγελοι του Σατανα. Και ο μεν εστι Κυριος απο αιωνων και εις τους αιωνας, ο δε αρχων καιρου του νυν της ανομιας.

xix.] Η ουν οδος του φωτος εστιν τοι αύτη. Εαν τις θελων οδον οδευειν επι τον ωρισμενον τοπον σπευση τοις εργοις αυτου. Εστιν ουν η δοθεισα[5] ημιν γνωσις του περιπατειν[6] εν ταυτη τοιαυτη. Αγαπησεις τον ποιησαντα σε, φοβηθηση τον σε πλασαντα, δοξασεις τον σε λυτρωσαμενον εκ θανατου. Εση απλους τη καρδια και πλουσιος τω πνευματι. Ου κολληθηση μετα πορευομενων εν οδω θανατου. Μισησεις παν ο ουκ εστιν αρεστον τω Θεω, μισησεις πασαν υποκρισιν. Ου μη εγκαταλιπης εντολας Κυριου. Ουκ υψωσεις σεαυτον, εση δε ταπεινοφρων[7] κατα παντα. Ουκ αρεις[8] επι σεαυτον δοξαν. Ου λημψη βουλην πονηραν κατα του πλησιον σου. Ου δωσεις τη ψυχη σου θρασος. Ου πορνευσεις, ου μοιχευσεις, ου παιδο-

In MS.:—[1] δηλωσε. [2] παραλελιπεναι. [3] νοησηται. [4] κεισθε.
[5] ιοθισα. [6] περιπατιν. [7] ταπινοφρων. [8] αρις.

youths.) The word of God shall not go out from thee with the impurity of certain persons. Thou shalt not take evil counsel. Thou shalt not accept persons when reproving any one for falling off [from the faith]. (Thou shalt be meek, thou shalt be gentle, thou shalt tremble at the words which thou hast heard.) Thou shalt not bear malice against thy brother. (Thou shalt not be of doubtful mind, whether a matter shall be or not*). Thou shalt not take the name of the Lord to a vain word. Thou shalt love thy neighbour as thyself. (Thou shalt not destroy a child by abortion, nor again shalt thou slay it when born.

Thou shalt not withdraw thy hand from thy son, or from thy daughter; but from childhood thou shalt teach them the fear of God) Thou shalt not be covetous of what is thy neighbour's. Thou shalt not be grasping; (nor shalt thou be joined in thy soul with the haughty, but thou shalt keep company with the lowly and the righteous.) (Thou shalt receive as good the difficulties which come upon thee, knowing that nothing comes to pass without God.) Thou shalt not be of two opinions, nor talkative. Thou shalt be subject to masters as to the image of God, in modesty and fear.) Thou shalt not give orders to thy slave or thy maid-servant in bitterness, since they trust in the same God; lest they shall not reverence the God who is over both; for he came not to call having respect to persons, but those for whom he had prepared the spirit. Thou shalt communicate in all things with thy neighbour, and thou shalt not call things thine own; for if ye are joint partakers of what is incorruptible, how much more of corruptible things! Thou shalt not be hasty with thy tongue; for the mouth is Death's snare.

* James, i. 8.

φθορησεις¹. Ου μη σου ο λογος του Θεου εξελθη εν ακαθαρσια τινων. Ου λημψη βουλην πονηραν. Ου λημψη προσωπον ελεγξαι² τινα επι παραπτωματι. Εση πραϋς, εση ησυχιος, εση τρεμων τους λογους ους ηκουσας. Ου μνησικακησεις τω αδελφω σου. Ου μη διψυχησεις ποτερον εσται η ου. Ου μη λαβης επι ματαιω το ονομα Κυριου. Αγαπησεις τον πλησιον σου ως εαυτον. Ου φονευσεις τεκνον εν φθορα, ουδε παλιν γεννηθεν αποκτενεις. Ου μη αρεις την χειρα σου απο του υιου σου, η απο της θυγατρος σου, αλλα απο νεοτητος διδαξεις φοβον Θεου. Ου μη γενη επιθυμων τα του πλησιον σου. Ου μη γενη πλεονεκτης, ουδε κολληθηση εκ ψυχης σου μετα υψηλων, αλλα μετα ταπεινων³ και δικαιων αναστραφηση. Τα συμβαινοντα σοι ενεργηματα ως αγαθα προσδεξη, ειδως οτι ανευ Θεου ουδεν γινεται⁴. Ουκ εση διγνωμων, ουδε γλωσσωδης. Υποταγη κυριοις ως τυπω Θεου αισχυνη και φοβω. Ου μη επιταξεις δουλω σου η παιδισκη εν πικρια, τοις επι τον αυτον Θεον ελπιζουσιν, μη ποτε ου μη φοβηθησονται τον επ' αμφοτεροις Θεον· ότι ουκ ηλθεν κατα προσωπον καλεσαι⁵, αλλ' εφ' ους το πνευμα ητοιμασεν. Κοινωνησεις εν πασιν τω πλησιον σου, και ουκ ερεις ιδια ειναι· ει γαρ εν τω αφθαρτω κοινωνοι εστε, ποσω μαλλον εν φθαρτοις; Ουκ εση προγλωσσος, παγις γαρ το στομα θανατου.

In MS.:—¹ παιδοφθορησις. ² ελεγξε. ³ ταπινων. ⁴ γεινεται. ⁵ καλεσε.

As far as possible thou shalt be pure in thy soul. Be not stretching forth thy hands to receive, while drawing back in giving.) Thou shalt love as the apple of thine eye every one that speaketh to thee the word of the Lord.) / Night and day thou shalt remember the day of judgment, and shalt seek every day the persons of the saints; either labouring at something by word and work and toil, and going forward to encourage, and meditating on saving a soul by the word; or through thy hands thou shalt work for the redemption of thy sins. / Thou shalt not hesitate to give; nor when giving shalt thou grumble. Give to every one that asketh of thee*, and thou wilt know who is the good recompenser of the reward. Thou shalt guard what thou hast received†, neither adding to it nor taking from it‡.

To the last thou shalt hate evil and shalt judge justly. Thou shalt not make a quarrel; thou shalt pacify those that fight, bringing them together; [God] will recognize it in thy sins. Thou shalt not go to prayer with an evil conscience. This is the way of light.

xx.] But the way of the Black one is full of crookedness and cursing; for it is an eternal way of death with punishment, in which are the things which destroy their souls—idolatry, over-confidence, arrogance of power, hypocrisy, double-heartedness, adultery, murder, rapine, haughtiness, transgressions, craft, malice, wilfulness, poisoning, want of fear of God. Persecutors of the good, hating truth, loving falsehood, not knowing the reward of righteousness, not cleaving to what is good, not attending to just judgment, nor to the widow and orphan, watching not in fear of God, but towards wickedness, men from whom meekness and

---

* Matt. v. 42. † 1 Tim. vi. 20. ‡ Comp. Rev. xxii. 18.

Οσον δυνασαι¹ υπερ της ψυχης σου αγνευσεις². Μη γινου³ προς μεν το λαβειν εκτεινων⁴ τας χειρας⁵, προς το δουναι συστελλων. Αγαπησεις ως κορην του οφθαλμου σου παντα τον λαλουντα σοι τον λογον Κυριου. Μνησθηση ημεραν κρισεως νυκτος και ημερας, και εκζητησεις καθ' εκαστην ημεραν τα προσωπα των αγιων, η δια λογου και εργου και κοπου κοπιων τι, και πορευομενος εις το παρακαλεσαι⁶, και μελετων εις το σωσαι ψυχην τῳ λογῳ, η δια των χειρων⁷ σου εργαση εις λυτρον αμαρτιων σου. Ου διστασεις⁸ δουναι, ουδε διδους γογγυσεις. Παντι τῳ αιτουντι σε διδου, γνωση δε τις ο του μισθου καλος ανταποδοτης. Φυλαξεις α παρελαβες, μητε προσθεις⁹, μητε αφαιρων.

Εις τελος μισησεις πονηρον, και κρινεις δικαιως. Ου ποιησεις σχισμα, ειρηνευσεις μαχομενους συναγαγων· εξομολογησει εν αμαρτιαις σου. Ου προσεξεις επι προσευχην εν συνειδησει¹⁰ πονηρᾳ. Αυτη εστιν η οδος του φωτος.

xx.] Η δε του Μελανος οδος εστιν σκολιας και καταρας μεστη· οδος γαρ εστιν θανατου αιωνια μετα τιμωριας, εν ῃ εστιν τα απολλυντα την ψυχην αυτων, ειδωλολατρεια¹¹, θρασυτης, υψος δυναμεως, υποκρισις, διπλοκαρδια, μοιχια, φονος, αρπαγη, υπερηφανια, παραβασεις, δολος, κακια, αυθαδια, φαρμακια, αφοβια Θεου. Διωκται των αγαθων, μισουντες αληθειαν¹², αγαπωντες ψευδη, ου γινωσκοντες μισθον δικαιοσυνης, ου κολλωμενοι αγαθῳ, ου κρισει δικαιᾳ, χηρᾳ και ορφανῳ ου προσεχοντες, αγρυπνουντες ουκ εις φοβ ν Θεου αλλα επι το πονηρον,

In MS.:—¹ ευνασε. ² αγνευσις. ³ γεινου. ⁴ εκτινων. ⁵ χιρας. ⁶ παρακαλεσε. ⁷ χιρων. ⁸ ειστασις. ⁹ προσθις. ¹⁰ συνιδεσει. ¹¹ ειδωλολατρια. ¹² αληθιαν.

patience are far off and at a distance, loving vanity, following after recompense, not pitying the poor man, not labouring for him that is overburdened, clever in slander, not knowing Him that made them, murderers of children, destroyers of God's workmanship, turning away him that is in want*, and oppressing him that is afflicted, advocates for the rich, unjust judges of the poor, doing wrong in all things.

xxi.] It is well for him who has learnt the judgments of the Lord, such as have been written, in them to walk. For he that keepeth these will be glorified in the kingdom of God. He that chooseth those [other] things will be destroyed together with his works. For the sake of this there will be a resurrection, for the sake of this a repayment. I beseech you the superiors, if ye receive any of my good knowledge, take counsel among yourselves towards whom ye shall carry it out; forsake not what is right. The day is at hand in which all things will perish together with the evil one. The Lord is at hand, and his reward. Again and again I beseech you, be good lawmakers to yourselves†, continue faithful counsellors for yourselves, take away from among you all hypocrisy.

And may God, who rules over all the world, give you wisdom, intelligence, understanding, knowledge of his judgments, patience. And be ye inquiring what the Lord requires of you, and perform it; so that ye may be found in the day of judgment. And if there is any good be careful to remember me, meditating on these things, so that [my] desire and watchfulness may result in some good. I beseech you, asking it as a favour, Until the noble Vessel [the body of Jesus] shall be with you, do not fail towards any one of

---

* Matt. v. 42.   † Comp. 1 Cor. vi. 1.

ὧν μακραν και πορρω πραΰτης και ὑπομονη, αγαπωντες ματαιοτητα, διωκοντες ανταποδομα, ουκ ελεωντες πτωχον, ου πονουντες επι καταπονουμενῳ, ευχερεις[1] εν καταλαλιᾳ, ου γινωσκοντες τον ποιησαντα αυτους, φονεις[2] τεκνων, φθορεις[3] πλασματος Θεου, αποστρεφομενοι τον ενδεομενον, και καταπονουντες τον θλιβομενον, πλουσιων παρακλητοι, πενητων ανομοι κριται, παντ' ἁμαρτητοι.

xxi.] Καλον εστιν μαθοντα τα δικαιωματα του Κυριου, ὁσα γεγραπται, εν τουτοις περιπατειν. Ὁ γαρ ταυτα ποιων εν τῃ βασιλειᾳ του Θεου δοξασθησεται· ὁ εκεινα εκλεγομενος μετα των εργων αὑτου συναπολειται[4]. Δια τουτο αναστασις, δια τουτο ανταποδομα. Ερωτω τους ὑπερεχοντας ει τινα μου γνωμης αγαθης λαμβανετε[5], συμβουλιαν εχετε μεθ' ἑαυτων εις οὑς εργασησθε· το καλον μη ενλειπητε[6]. Εγγυς ἡ ἡμερα εν ᾑ συναπολειται[7] παντα τῳ πονηρῳ. Εγγυς ὁ Κυριος και ὁ μισθος αυτου. Ετι και ετι ερωτω ὑμας, ἑαυτων γινεσθε[8] νομοθεται αγαθων, ἑαυτων μενετε συμβουλοι πιστοι, αρατε[9] εξ ὑμων πασαν ὑποκρισιν.

Ὁ δε Θεος, ὁ του παντος κοσμου κυριευων, δῴη ὑμιν σοφιαν, συνεσιν, επιστημην, γνωσιν των δικαιωματων αυτου, ὑπομονην. Γιγνεσθε δε εκζητουντες τι ζητει[10] Κυριος αφ' ὑμων, και ποιειτε[11], ἱνα εὑρεθητε[12] εν ἡμερᾳ κρισεως. Ει δε τι εστιν αγαθον, μνειᾳ[13] μνημονευετε[14] μου, μελετωντες ταυτα, ἱνα και ἡ επιθυμια και ἡ αγρυπνια εις τι αγαθον χωρησῃ. Ερωτω ὑμας χαριν αιτουμενος, 'Εως ετι το καλον Σκευος εστιν[15] μεθ' ὑμων μη ενλειπητε[16].

In MS.:—[1] ευχερις.   [2] φονις.   [3] φθορις.   [4] συναπολιται.
[5] λαμβανεται.   [6] ενλιπηται.   [7] συναπολιται.   [8] γεινεσθαι.
[9] αραται.   [10] ζητι.   [11] ποιειται.   [12] ευρεθηται.   [13] μνια.
[14] μνημονευεται.   [15] Conj. εσται.   [16] ενλιπηται.

yourselves, but seek these things earnestly, and fulfil every command; for this is fitting. ' Wherefore I have the more hastened to write from where I was able to be safe, in order to cheer you. Children of love and peace, may the Lord of glory and of all grace be with your spirit.

The Epistle of Barnabas.

μηδενι εαυτων, αλλα συνεχως εκζητειτε[1] ταυτα, και αναπληρουτε[2] πασαν εντολην· εστιν γαρ αξιον. Διο μαλλον εσπουδασα γραψαι[3] αφ' ων ηδυνηθην, εις το ευφραναι ύμας, σωζεσθαι. Αγαπης τεκνα και ειρηνης[4], ό Κυριος της δοξης και πασης χαριτος μετα του πνευματος ύμων.

ΕΠΙΣΤΟΛΗ
ΒΑΡΝΑ
ΒΑ.

In MS.:—[1] εκζητιται. [2] αναπληρουται. [3] γραψε. [4] ιρηνης.

WORKS BY THE TRANSLATOR.

The Holy Bible translated, being a revision of the Authorized English Version.

The Book of Isaiah, arranged chronologically in a revised translation and with historical notes.

Short Notes to accompany a revised translation of the Hebrew Scriptures.

The New Testament, translated from Griesbach's Text. Thirteenth thousand.

Critical Notes on the Authorised English Version of the New Testament. Second Edition.

The History of the Hebrew Nation and its Literature. Third Edition.

Texts from the Holy Bible explained by the help of the Ancient Monuments. Second Edition.

The History of Egypt from the Earliest Times till the Conquest by the Arabs in A.D. 640. Sixth Edition.

Alexandrian Chronology.

Egyptian Inscriptions from the British Museum and other Sources. 216 Plates in folio.

Egyptian Hieroglyphics; being an Attempt to explain their Nature, Origin, and Meaning. With a Vocabulary.

Egyptian Antiquities in the British Museum described.

Egyptian Mythology and Egyptian Christianity; with their Influence on the Opinions of Modern Christendom.

The Decree of Canopus in Hieroglyphics and Greek.

The Rosetta Stone in Hieroglyphics and Greek.

Hebrew Inscriptions from the Valleys between Egypt and Mount Sinai in their original characters, with translations and an alphabet. Parts I. and II.

The Chronology of the Bible.

A Short Hebrew Grammar without points.

The Book Genesis I.-XVIII. and XX.-XXV. 10, without points, and with prefixes and suffixes detached.

The Journeys and Epistles of the Apostle Paul. Third Edition.

An Inquiry into the Age of the Moabite Stone.

www.ingramcontent.com/pod-product-compliance
Lightning Source LLC
Chambersburg PA
CBHW032250080426
42735CB00008B/1080